James Woodward is a Ca
extensively in the area of p
recent publications include
Older People (SPCK, 2008). He is particularly interested in how Christian discipleship nurtures and deepens human well-being. For further information about his work, see his website <www.jameswoodward.info>.

Paula Gooder is a freelance writer and lecturer in biblical studies. She is also a Reader in the Diocese of Birmingham and Canon Theologian of Birmingham and Guildford Cathedrals, as well as a lay Canon of Salisbury Cathedral. Her recent publications include *Searching for Meaning: An Introduction to Interpreting the New Testament* (SPCK, 2008) and *Heaven* (SPCK, 2011).

Mark Pryce is Bishop's Adviser for Clergy Continuing Ministerial Education in the Diocese of Birmingham. His other publications include the *Literary Companion to the Lectionary* (2001) and the *Literary Companion for Festivals: Readings for Commemorations Throughout the Year* (2003), both published by SPCK.

JOURNEYING WITH MARK

Lectionary Year B

James Woodward, Paula Gooder
and Mark Pryce

First published in Great Britain in 2011

Society for Promoting Christian Knowledge
36 Causton Street
London SW1P 4ST
www.spckpublishing.co.uk

British Library Cataloguing-in-Publication Data
A catalogue record for this book is available from the British Library

ISBN 978–0–281–05901–0
eBook ISBN 978–0–281–06680–3

Typeset by Graphicraft Ltd, Hong Kong
First printed in Great Britain by MPG Books Group
Subsequently digitally printed in Great Britain

Produced on paper from sustainable forests

This book is dedicated to Christopher Evans in his hundredth year: priest, scholar and Birmingham boy, with our love and respect

Contents

Preface: What is this book about?

The Revised Common Lectionary has established itself in Anglican parishes (and in other denominations) as the framework within which the Bible is read on Sundays in public worship. It follows a three-year pattern, taking each of the synoptic Gospels and reading substantial parts of them in the cycle of the liturgical year. While each of the three years is dedicated in turn to readings from Matthew, Mark and Luke, during parts of the year extensive use is also made of John.

All three authors of the present book have extensive experience of reading, preaching, leading, learning and teaching within this framework. We have worked in a variety of contexts: universities, theological colleges, parishes, chaplaincies and religious communities. We share a passion for theological learning that is collaborative, inclusive, intelligent and transformative. This shared concern brought us together across our participation in various aspects of the life of the Diocese of Birmingham in 2007, and we started a conversation about how best we might help individuals and groups understand and use the Gospels. We aspired to provide a short resource for Christians with busy and distracted lives so that the Gospel narrative might be explained, illuminated and interpreted for discipleship and service. This first volume about Mark (further volumes dealing with Matthew and Luke will follow) is the result of the writers' conversations and reflects the growth in our understanding of this remarkable text. We attended to Mark's text and examined how best to break open the character of the Gospel. We wanted to offer a mixture of information, interpretation and reflection on life experience in the light of faith.

Our own text has emerged out of shared study and reflection. We have all been able to comment and shape each other's contributions. We hope that the material will be used in whatever way might help the learning life of disciples and communities of faith. We expect that some of the material might be used as a base for study days and preparation for teaching and preaching.

But this book is about more than offering information and resources for the busy Christian who might want a prompt for worship or teaching. We hope that this book will enable readers (alone or in groups) to enter into the shape of Mark's Gospel; to enter imaginatively into its life, its concerns, its message; and in doing so to follow the particular demands of discipleship presented to us by the Gospel writer. We want you to use it as a springboard for imagination. The people and events of the Gospels become more concrete and vivid for us when we try to bring them to life before our eyes. We want to try to get inside the skin of how the Gospel of Mark gives shape to the story of Jesus and what it asks of us today about how we might follow him. Visualizing the backdrop to the lives, the times and the culture of first-century Israel is like setting the stage in a play. We want you to pay attention to the details that Mark has supplied. We aim to place the Gospel account in its setting so we can enliven our perception of what happened and expand our understanding of the landscape within which the grace of God acts.

As we reconstruct the scene in our imagination we want to apply our mind to considering its meaning. We ask what truth is revealed and highlighted through it. We pray that the Holy Spirit will help us all to grow in comprehension and appreciation of the practical and spiritual realities demonstrated in the text of Mark. Imagination and understanding are part of deepening our encounter with Christ. And with a heart of love we can become more responsive to his word of love to us.

A short volume such as this can make no claim to comprehensiveness. The criteria for our choice of seasons and texts were determined by our attention to the liturgical year. Our choice has also been shaped by our attempt to present some of the key characteristics of the Gospel.

The Introduction offers a concise exploration of the main characteristics and themes of Mark's Gospel. Paula Gooder helps us into the Gospel through a discussion of Mark's style of writing, the characters he depicts and the shape of the overall narrative, and considers how we might see the mission and ministry of Jesus within the context of the story that Mark tells us. We look at the nature of the good news that Mark shares with us, especially in the light of the cross and the way of the cross. Finally we consider the context within which the Gospel was written and reflect on what we know about the person of Mark himself.

The Introduction is completed with a piece of poetry written by Mark Pryce, who invites us into the transforming power of Jesus and explores how that power might continue to unfold in our lives.

A similar pattern is followed in the subsequent seven chapters, each of which picks up one of the major seasons in the cycle of the Church's liturgical year. In the section headed 'Exploring the text', Paula offers us material to expound the particular style of the Gospel. In the section 'Imagining the text', Mark Pryce's theology is distilled in poetry and prose, offering us imaginative spiritual insights grounded in the Gospel messages. He draws for these on many of the set readings for the Lectionary year of Mark, as they help us to understand the Gospel within the seasonal cycle of the Christian year. These imaginative pieces can be used in services as reflective material for sermons or meditation. James completes these sections with 'Reflecting on the text', in which he offers some pastoral and practical theological reflections that hold together faith and experience. At the end of each chapter, in a section headed 'Action, conversation, questions, prayer', we ask readers to consider the foregoing material in the light of their own understanding and experience. These questions might form the basis of group conversation and study.

Throughout we have tried to wear our scholarship lightly so that the book may be both accessible and stimulating. At the end of the book we offer some resources for further learning.

We hope that you will find this book useful and that it will give you a glimpse of how much we have gained from our collaboration on this project. As individuals we write and work in different ways and this, combined with James's change of ministry in 2009, has caused some delays in the meeting of our deadlines. We thank Ruth McCurry, our editor, for her trust and forbearance. We also thank all those people and communities that have enriched, informed and challenged our responses to Mark's Gospel.

James Woodward
Paula Gooder
Mark Pryce

Introduction: Getting to know the Gospel of Mark

Exploring the text

Mark's Gospel is probably the best known of all the Gospels. There is something about its lively, punchy style that draws us right into the story it is telling. Mark's Gospel, more than any other, encourages us to enter imaginatively into the world of Jesus: to walk with Jesus and his disciples, to feel the anger of the authorities and the wonder of the crowd, to see Jesus' miracles and hear his preaching. Mark's style of writing is vivid (he uses the phrase 'and immediately' more than any other Gospel writer), fresh and animated. It draws us into its story and encourages us, who read it in the twenty-first century, to respond to 'the good news of Jesus Christ, the Son of God' (Mark 1.1) just as much as it did its readers in the first century.

Mark's style of writing

One very noticeable characteristic of Mark's Gospel is its attention to detail. Mark invariably provides much more detailed description of events than either Matthew or Luke. A famous example of this is Mark's account of the feeding of the five thousand:

> But he answered them, 'You give them something to eat.' *They said to him, 'Are we to go and buy two hundred denarii worth of bread, and give it to them to eat?' And he said to them, 'How many loaves have you? Go and see.' When they had found out,* they said, 'Five, and two fish.' Then he ordered them to get all the people to sit down in groups on the *green* grass. So they sat down in

> groups of *hundreds and of* fifties. Taking the five loaves and the two fish, he looked up to heaven, and blessed and broke the loaves, and gave them to his disciples to set before the people; *and he divided the two fish among them all.* And all ate and were filled; and they took up twelve baskets full of broken pieces and of the fish. Those who had eaten the loaves numbered five thousand men. (Mark 6.37–44)

The words in italic type here include what is in Mark's account of the feeding but not in the versions given by Matthew and Luke. Even a swift glance at the words in italic tells us that Mark gives much more detail. He tells us for example that the grass upon which the people sat was green (v. 39). This may seem an unnecessary level of information until we remember that at certain times of the year the grass would have been brown. As a result this is not superfluous detail, but may tell us what time of year is being referred to. Mark also fills in much more of the conversation between Jesus and the disciples and from it we gain a greater sense of their frustration and anxiety. He also gives more detail on the differing sizes of the groups who sat down and on what he did to the fish.

While none of this detail is absolutely necessary, it fills in gaps in the story, making the account more vivid as though an eyewitness has observed the events and is telling them to us. Mark's love of detail means that, although his Gospel is the shortest of the four (16 chapters for Mark, 28 for Matthew, 24 for Luke and 21 for John), whenever one of Mark's stories is placed next to its equivalent from Matthew or Luke (as we have done with the story of the feeding of the five thousand), Mark's account is nearly always longer. Mark's Gospel is shorter because he includes fewer stories, but those that he does include are told in a little more detail. This detail invites us to enter the story and to feel as though we too are present alongside the eyewitness who tells it to us.

The characters of Mark's Gospel

Another feature of Mark's Gospel is that the characters are vividly drawn. It is particularly interesting to notice that three groups of people ('the authorities', 'the crowd' and 'the disciples') appear regularly in the story. And when they appear, they often (though not always) react to Jesus in a consistent way.

- The authorities – who are variously the priests and chief priests, the Pharisees, the scribes and the Sadducees – are opposed to Jesus from the start. They are suspicious, argumentative and generally antagonistic to Jesus and his ministry.
- The crowd appears more consistently in Mark than in any other Gospel and its members are often amazed by Jesus (see, for example, Mark 1.27; 2.12; 5.20). They are impressed by his teaching and his miracles but never seem able to take a step beyond amazement at what he says and does.
- The disciples are the group which, for obvious reasons, we encounter most often in Mark's Gospel and yet they receive a very bad press. In Mark's Gospel the disciples regularly fail to understand Jesus; they ask stupid questions, fail to understand the answers and ultimately run away, leaving Jesus alone. They often seem almost to understand him but, crucially, fail to do so when it matters most. (For more on the disciples see Chapter 6.)

These characteristics are well illustrated by the story about the healing of the man who was paralysed and let down to Jesus on a mat by his friends. Here the authorities are represented by the scribes, who sit there questioning how it is that Jesus can say and do what he does; whereas the crowd who have pressed into the house to hear Jesus are amazed and glorify God.

> Now some of the *scribes* were sitting there, questioning in their hearts, 'Why does this fellow speak in this way? It is blasphemy!

> Who can forgive sins but God alone?' . . . And he stood up, and immediately took the mat and went out before *all of them*; so that *they were all amazed and glorified God, saying, 'We have never seen anything like this!'* Jesus went out again beside the lake; the *whole crowd gathered around him, and he taught them.* (Mark 2.6–7, 12–13)

The effect of the way in which Mark portrays these characters is not just to draw us into the story but to challenge us into responding ourselves. Will we, like the authorities, remain sceptical and opposed to Jesus? Will we, like the crowd, express our wonder but do nothing more than that? Will we, like the disciples, follow Jesus but never really grasp who he was or what he came to do? Or will we, like the ragbag collection of outsiders that Jesus met over and over again, come as we are and respond to him as he is?

The whole of Mark's Gospel

One of the great challenges presented by Mark's Gospel is to find a way of reading it so that we get the best out of it. The characteristics that we have already noted appear most clearly when Mark is read from beginning to end. In fact it is the reading of the whole Gospel that brings to the fore Mark's love of detail and the stereotypical character of the groups we looked at above. It is only when we find the authorities or the crowd reacting again in the same way as they did a few verses or chapters ago that the patterns of Mark's Gospel begin to build up.

Mark is a complete Gospel narrative and works best when read in one go, from beginning to end. When we read it that way we get a sense of the pace of the Gospel, of the way in which the shadow of the cross hangs over Jesus' life and ministry, of the odd mystery of Jesus' command to so many people not to tell others about him, and, parallel with that, of God's dramatic revelations of who Jesus is at his baptism and transfiguration. Only when we read it from beginning to end do we begin to understand a bit more of what Mark is trying to do in his Gospel.

This poses something of a challenge to churches and individuals alike. It is simply not possible – nor desirable – to read the whole of Mark every week, and yet it is good to attempt to get some sort of overview of it. Reading the whole Gospel as a group, or finding people to perform it, can be an excellent way of getting ready to hear its message.

Keeping an overview of Mark's Gospel in mind

It is also helpful to have an overview of the Gospel in mind when hearing or reading a particular passage. There are many different ways of splitting Mark's Gospel into an outline, but the one I find most helpful for understanding the whole sweep of the Gospel is to divide it into four sections:

1 Jesus' ministry (1.2—4.34)
2 Discipleship and responses to Jesus (4.35—8.26)
3 The way of the cross (8.27—10.52)
4 Jesus' journey to the cross (11.1—end)

The value of this outline is that it is relatively easy to remember (approximately four chapters per section), so it is quite straightforward to work out from a verse reference which section the passage falls into. The other value is that this outline recognizes the fact that Mark's Gospel works its way up to a climax at the crucifixion of Jesus.

Jesus' ministry (1.2—4.34)

The first section of Mark's Gospel sets up the nature and character of Jesus' ministry. In it we find

- the revelation by God of who Jesus is at Jesus' baptism (1.2–15), coupled with later commands to keep this identity secret (1.44–45; 3.12);
- the calling of the disciples (1.16–22; 2.14), and sending them out to proclaim the good news (3.13–19);

- five specific healings:
  - one of a man possessed by a demon (1.21–28)
  - one of Simon's mother-in-law (1.29–31)
  - one of a leper who aroused Jesus' pity (1.40–45)
  - one of a paralysed man (2.1–12)
  - one of a man with a withered hand (3.1–5)
  - plus general healings (1.34; 3.9–12);
- the need for Jesus to withdraw because of his popularity (1.35–39);
- the growing opposition of the leaders to Jesus' ministry (2.6–12, 15–17, 23–28; 3.1–6);
- different forms of teaching by Jesus:
  - teaching about fasting and wineskins (2.18–22)
  - teaching about the nature of families and Beelzebul (3.21–35)
  - a parable about sowing seed, with a private explanation to the disciples (4.1–34).

In almost four chapters, then, Mark sets the tone for Jesus' ministry. In these chapters we meet a person who heals extensively and teaches in a variety of ways, who calls disciples and sends them out to proclaim good news, and who becomes popular with the crowd and the enemy of the authorities. These strands set out the themes of Jesus' ministry which can, in Mark's Gospel, be traced throughout the whole of his life.

Discipleship and responses to Jesus (4.35—8.26)

The second section of Mark's Gospel includes many of the strands set up in the first section but focuses on one in particular. The theme of discipleship and of responding to Jesus comes to the fore in this section. One of the striking features of this section of Mark is the scenes set in a boat. Three such scenes feature at intervals throughout the section:

- 4.35–41 contains the story of Jesus' stilling of the storm;
- 6.45–52 tells the account of Jesus walking on the water while the disciples rowed across the Sea of Galilee;
- 8.14–21 recounts the somewhat odd discussion between Jesus and his disciples about the leaven of the Pharisees, which the disciples misunderstand as a rebuke about whether they have brought bread or not.

In all three of these accounts an issue arises about the disciples' response to Jesus.

- In the story of the stilling of the storm the disciples become afraid of the one who can control the wind and sea (4.41).
- In the account of Jesus' walking on water, the disciples are astounded by Jesus and do not understand (6.52).
- And in the third narrative, where we find the discussion about the leaven of the Pharisees, the full extent of the disciples' lack of comprehension comes to the fore (8.14–21).

This second section, then, not only begins and ends with the disciples' lack of comprehension of Jesus, it also includes a further episode right in the middle which focuses on the same theme. Many people seek to defend the disciples at this point, noting that they remained with Jesus even though they didn't entirely understand who he was. This is of course true, but if we look at how Mark treats these issues it seems as though by telling the story as it does, the Gospel seeks to lay down a challenge to its hearers.

We noticed above that the responses of the three main groups of characters – the authorities, the crowd and the disciples – to Jesus may have been particularly portrayed by Mark so as to elicit a response from the readers of the Gospel about how they will respond to Jesus. Another feature that may support this theory is the individuals who meet Jesus between the three iconic boat scenes. In between the accounts of the stilling of the storm and the walking on the water, Jesus meets a man possessed by demons who lives in the region of the Gerasenes (5.1–20), Jairus, whose daughter has died, and a woman who is haemorrhaging blood (5.21–43). In between the narrative of Jesus walking on the water and the discussion about leaven in the boat, he meets a Syrophoenician woman whose daughter is ill (7.24–30) and a deaf man (7.31–37). Finally, immediately after that last boat scene, Jesus meets a blind man from Bethsaida (8.22–26).

Each of these accounts features an individual who – with the exception of Jairus – lives on the outskirts of his or her society and who recognizes in Jesus a response to his or her deep need. It would be facile to say these people understood Jesus better than the disciples, but each one of them seemed to understand something of the one who could give them what they needed so much. Each one of these people responds to Jesus from the depths of his or her being and brings into focus the theme of this section.

The way of the cross (8.27—10.52)

The third section, the shortest of the four, builds on the second section. In section two the theme seems to be response. In section three it is responsibility. In this section the shadow of the cross falls even more powerfully over the Gospel than it has done up to this point. Here the question of the identity of Jesus gains momentum. Jesus is acknowledged by Peter to be the Messiah (8.27–33) and is revealed as God's Son in the transfiguration (9.1–9), but woven around this is Jesus' identity in his vocation. In this third section Jesus' prophecies about his suffering and death become more and more important, until we begin to see that his suffering and death are as much about who he is as are his Messiah-ship and Son-ship.

Also important is the revelation that the way of the cross is not for Jesus alone. Those who respond to Jesus and become his followers must be prepared to follow him to the cross. With response comes responsibility. We who respond must also be prepared to take up our crosses as we follow in the footsteps of Jesus.

Jesus' journey to the cross (11.1—end)

The final section of Mark's Gospel turns its attention to the last week of Jesus' life. The significance of the cross in Mark can be noted simply in mathematical terms: nearly a third of this short Gospel is concerned with the last week of Jesus' life and the events that lead him, ultimately, to the cross. In these final six chapters the tension builds and builds until Jesus fulfils his calling and dies . . . and is recognized to be God's Son by the Roman centurion who ensured his death.

The beginning of the good news

The alert reader will have noticed that the outline for Mark's Gospel given above began at 1.2, not at 1.1. This is because there is some discussion about the role of 1.1 in the Gospel. Mark's Gospel begins simply with the words, 'The beginning of the good news of Jesus Christ, the Son of God' (1.1). One of the questions that arises from this is whether it is simply a way into the story and the opposite of the announcement of 'the end' which is often used to end fairy tales, or whether it tells us something about the nature of the Gospel. Either is possible.

If this verse is not just a statement that the Gospel has begun, then it may refer not only to 1.1 but to the whole Gospel. It is possible that 'the beginning' refers to the fact that Mark's Gospel recounts the beginning of the good news of Jesus Christ but nothing more than that. The rest of the story of the good news of Jesus Christ is to be told in the lives and responses of those who read the Gospel.

Getting to know the person of Mark

The task of getting to know the Gospel of Mark is relatively straightforward. We have all the evidence we need in front of us – all we have to do is to become familiar with it. Unfortunately getting to know the 'Mark' who wrote the Gospel is much more complex, since the evidence is scant and hard to find.

It is an obvious thing to say – but nevertheless quite important to remind ourselves – that the Gospels are stories about Jesus and not about the Gospel writers. All the Gospel writers fulfil their task so well that it is, in fact, quite hard to work out anything about who wrote the Gospels, when and why. Nevertheless we, as twenty-first-century readers, want to know a little more about who these people were, why they wrote the Gospels and when they did it. As a result we must dig around to find evidence that may help answer our questions. It is important to remember, however, that our quest runs slightly contrary to the aims of the Gospel writers themselves, who wanted to introduce us to Jesus not to themselves, and that it therefore cannot be guaranteed any level of success.

We can tell a little about the author of the Gospel of Mark from the pages of the Gospel itself, and it is worth collecting this evidence together at the start. The author of Mark has a vivid, immediate style which suggests an eyewitness testimony, and yet he sometimes gets the immediate geography and customs of Galilee slightly wrong. So, for example, in the account of the healing of the man in Gerasa from a demon, Mark implies in 5.1 and 5.13 that Gerasa was right on the shores of Lake Galilee, whereas it is a few miles inland and south of Lake Galilee. Similarly, Mark 7.31 talks about a journey from Tyre, through Sidon, to Galilee, whereas Sidon is north of Tyre and Galilee south, so it would be hard to travel through Sidon from Tyre to the Galilee. This suggests therefore that though the author of Mark's Gospel received his information from an eyewitness, he was not an eyewitness himself.

Other evidence suggests that Mark's Gospel was written into a context which itself was not Jewish – or not entirely Jewish – and which seems more Roman in origin. For example, in 7.3–4

Mark gives a brief explanation of the Jewish customs of cleansing before eating. The implication of this is that his audience wouldn't otherwise have understood the conversation about cleanliness that Jesus had with the Pharisees. Also interesting is the fact that Mark puts the Latin names for things (e.g. his reference to the centurion in 15.39) into Greek letters; this suggests that he, or his audience, or both, were familiar with Latin as well as Greek.

The only other evidence for the authorship of the Gospel comes from outside the New Testament. In the second century AD, Papias of Hierapolis attributed the Gospel to Mark, who, he said, was an interpreter of Peter and who wrote down carefully, though not in order, all of Peter's memories of Jesus. (What Papias said no longer remains, but Eusebius quoted him as saying this in his *History of the Church*, 3.39.15.) This tradition is supported by a number of early writers, including Irenaeus, Origen, Tertullian and Clement of Alexandria. Most of these early Christian writers also claim that Mark wrote the Gospel before the death of Peter (Peter is thought to have died in Nero's persecutions in AD 64 or 65). The only exception is Irenaeus, who appears to claim that Peter had died by the time Mark wrote the Gospel.

What is unclear, however, is who Mark was. Church tradition has various different explanations of his identity. In various places Mark has been associated with John Mark (who is referred to in the Acts of the Apostles) and with Mark the brother of Barnabas, though others maintain that he was one of the 70 originally sent out by Jesus in Luke 10.1. Most modern scholars would not be convinced by any of these associations, on the grounds, noted above, that the author does not seem completely familiar with the geography of Palestine, which suggests that he did not himself live there. In reality the name Mark was popular in the Roman world and could refer to any number of people. As a result the precise identity of Mark will probably never be known.

We shouldn't leave the question of Mark's identity without noting the tradition that the author of Mark was the young man in the garden of Gethsemane who followed Jesus in nothing but a linen cloth and who ran away naked when they tried to catch him. Sadly there is no evidence for this at all, but it remains a romantic explanation that appeals to many.

Getting to know the context of Mark

Our final exploration into Mark concerns when the Gospel might have been written. Again the evidence for this is scant and frustratingly vague. We have already noted that some early Church fathers think that it was written before the death of Peter, whereas others – notably Irenaeus – say that it was after Peter's death. Many modern scholars would place its date between around AD 65 and 75 (i.e. after Peter's death but not long afterwards). This is because Mark's Gospel is widely regarded not only as the first to be written but as the one which was used as a source by Matthew and Luke when they wrote their Gospels. If this is the case, then Mark would need to have been written and had time to become widely accepted by the early Christians before Matthew and Luke were written. This pushes the date more towards AD 65–75.

There is little agreement, however, about whether Mark's Gospel was written before or after the destruction of the temple in AD 70. This was a particularly significant time in Jewish history when, after a rebellion by the Jews and a subsequent hard-fought battle that took place some time between AD 67 and 70, the Jews were defeated by the Romans and their temple destroyed. This action significantly changed the nature of Judaism for ever and marks a watershed period in the first century. Many New Testament texts were written around this period as a response to the events that took place in Palestine. Some scholars think that Mark 13 was written in expectation that the Jews would be defeated, others that it was written after then and reflects the trauma of a people who have seen the temple destroyed.

It is impossible to tell from the available evidence which is the correct date. What does seem likely, however, is that Mark – like all the Gospels – was written in order to ensure that the stories about Jesus did not die with the people who told them. Mark's Gospel was written down to make sure that this was, in fact, only the beginning of the good news of Jesus – and not the end of it. Who wrote it, and when, has faded into the mists of time, but the Gospel remains today as vibrant and challenging as it was when first written down nearly two millennia ago.

Imagining the text

The following poem traces, in an imaginary way, how a Gospel such as Mark might have taken shape out of the remembered experience of the first disciples, who find a story worth telling as the significance of the teaching, death and resurrection of Jesus begins to dawn in their hearts and minds. Mark's Gospel begins this telling of 'the good news of Jesus Christ, the Son of God' by recounting how those who first encountered Jesus were changed by their experience of him. The good news of the Gospel continues to unfold in the lives of those who hear this story of Jesus and are transformed by it – a living and dynamic message, not just personal memories.

The poem makes reference to a number of incidents and dimensions within Mark's Gospel. For example: Jesus calling the disciples (1.14–20, 3 before Advent); the nature of discipleship (8.34–37, Lent 2, Proper 19; 10.41–45, Proper 24); Jesus' healing ministry (3.1–6, Proper 4; 5.21–43, Proper 8); the imagery and style of Jesus' teaching (4.26–34, Proper 6; 9.42–49, Proper 21; 13.28–29, Advent 1).

Peter and the others begin to see things differently . . .

Once we got ourselves safely back to Galilee
Expecting to resume business as usual
Out on the water without him,
Casting and hauling, sorting and selling,
It was then we recognized what he had done for us.

He was a man who paid attention,
Observing detail
With a careful eye for the small difference:
'Look at the fig tree,' he would say,
Tracing its tender branches,
Teaching us to feel for buds,
To sense an expectation of summer.

The secret growth of seeds,
The nesting habit of birds in certain shrubs,
The inner qualities of yeast, of salt,
None of these mysteries evaded him.
Like a farmer, like a mother,
He watched the wisdom of each shift
In growth and in diminishment,
To find in them
God's quiet ecology of kingdom.

And just as he had drawn us once
From scores of fishermen along the beach,
So now we find ourselves noticing others, getting involved –
Like him we see the children,
We sense the withered hand, the concealed wound in the crowd –
Like him we shape our lives around the hidden work of service;
We find that we are carrying the heavy weight of his cross.

Action, conversation, questions, prayer

In this introductory chapter we have opened ourselves up to some ideas about the context in which Mark's Gospel was written, the issues it addressed and the ways in which it may have emerged from the experience of the early disciples. The following activities will help us to begin deepening our understanding.

Action

We suggest that you take some time to read the whole of Mark's Gospel in one sitting.

Conversation and questions

- What is the context within which you read Mark's Gospel?
- What are the events, characteristics, values which shape your context?
- What impact of Jesus on your life/community has taken time for you to recognize or understand?
- What images that Jesus uses in Mark's Gospel strike you particularly?

Prayer

Blessed Lord, who hast caused all holy Scriptures to be written for our learning; Grant that we may in such wise hear them, read, mark, learn, and inwardly digest them, that by patience, and comfort of thy holy Word, we may embrace, and ever hold fast the blessed hope of everlasting life, which thou hast given us in our Saviour Jesus Christ. Amen.

The Book of Common Prayer

1

Advent

Exploring the text

The season of Advent is about waiting, both for the Jesus who came to earth as a baby and for the victorious, risen and ascended Christ who will return to earth as King. One of the challenges of Advent is to keep our vision fixed not only on the more tangible and comprehensible birth of Jesus but also on Jesus' second coming. Mark's Gospel naturally focuses our vision on the second coming because, unlike the Gospels of Matthew and Luke, it has no stories of Jesus' birth. Mark simply begins with the adult Jesus starting his ministry with his baptism in the Jordan. The Gospel does, however, contain a passage – Mark 13 – which has been one of the most significant in discussions about Jesus' second coming.

Mark 13: Waiting for the Son of Man

Mark 13 begins with an apparently specific conversation about the fate of the temple, but from there moves outwards into a description of general chaos and lawlessness. This builds to a climax in verse 24 where the natural world begins to reflect the chaos of the human world, when the sun is darkened and stars begin falling from heaven. At this point we are told that the Son of Man will come 'in clouds with great power and glory' (13.26). The whole chapter ends with a warning about the importance of keeping alert, and of being able to read the signs of the times and understand what is happening. This is one of the most complex passages of Mark's Gospel, and one of the most difficult to understand. Indeed it is so difficult that there is very little agreement among scholars about what it refers to or what it means.

Interpreting Mark 13 in terms of the past or the future?

One of the hardest things to work out about Mark 13 is what events are being referred to. The traditional interpretation of the passage is that the events described by Jesus in Mark 13 all refer to the glorious second coming of Jesus, when the Son of Man (i.e. Jesus) will come back to earth on the clouds in glory. This event is often called by scholars the *Parousia*, which is simply the Greek word for 'arrival' or 'coming'. Mark 13 has, for much of Christian history, been considered to be Jesus' own prophecy of the end of the world and of the events that will signal his return, and this is a view that remains popular among many contemporary interpreters. Some interpreters try to make connections between this chapter (along with other key passages from the New Testament like Revelation) and events in the modern world, in order to predict when Jesus' return might take place.

Other scholars view the passage as either primarily or entirely referring to the events surrounding the destruction of Jerusalem in AD 70. Thus the events described in the passage are not to be seen as signals of the 'end of the world', but of the end of the world as the Jews knew it in AD 70, when their temple was destroyed and many Jews were driven out of Jerusalem. In this interpretation the events prophesied by Jesus are tied up with specific historical events from the first century and are understood in the light of what happened during this traumatic period of Jewish history. Still other scholars take a halfway position, and consider some of the chapter (particularly the first part) to be about the destruction of Jerusalem and the rest to be looking further into the future.

It is almost impossible to adjudicate between these positions: they all have their passionate advocates and they all use the text to interpret events in history. The difference is that some use the text to interpret the first century, others to interpret the twenty-first century, and yet others to look far into the future.

Mark 13 and Jewish apocalyptic literature

Many people find the complexity of the passage and the disagreements between interpreters so off-putting that they prefer to skip the chapter and all it represents. To do this, however, is to lose something of worth.

One of the reasons why Mark 13 sounds so odd to our twenty-first-century ears is because it is steeped in Jewish apocalyptic literature. Indeed for many years this chapter was called 'the Little Apocalypse', because many scholars thought that the whole chapter began life as a Jewish Christian piece of apocalyptic writing. This is now no longer so widely accepted, but it does remind us of how important it is to recognize that this chapter – like so much of the New Testament – can only be really understood in the light of all the other Jewish apocalyptic writings that exist both inside the Bible (here the significant writings are Daniel and Revelation) and outside (with books like *1 Enoch* or parts of the Dead Sea Scrolls).

One of the key features of Jewish apocalyptic literature is a strong belief in the connection that exists between earth and heaven. What this means is that the writers of this kind of material believed passionately that God intervenes in the course of history and that it was important to understand the events of earth in the light of this belief. Odd as it may seem to us, the fantastical language and the grim prophecies of doom and disaster were intended to offer a ray of hope to the readers of the texts. This kind of passage was intended to offer comfort in the midst of terror and despair. When Mark's readers found themselves with the world, as they knew it, falling apart, they were to remember the words of Jesus and to lift their eyes beyond the immediate events of this world to the one – the Son of Man – who had come once to this world and had promised to return.

Mark 13 and Advent

However we interpret the words of Mark 13, the season of Advent reminds us of the chapter's major point, that whatever it might feel like now, we are not abandoned. In many ways our world today feels more ordered and controlled than the ancient world, but not always. In our lives, just as the ancients did, we encounter things we cannot control – natural disasters, terrorism, illness, fear – and the message of Mark 13 is as relevant to us as it was to Mark's original readers. Disaster may come but we should not allow our panic to drive us to accept as Messiah someone who cannot save us (v. 21). In the face of things falling apart – even if this involves something as dramatic as stars falling from heaven – we should remember that Jesus' words are sure and reliable (v. 31). No matter how bleak things get, we should remember that beyond our sight God has not forgotten us. Mark 13 ends with a reminder that we do not know when the master of the house will come (v. 35). This is certainly true, nor indeed are we very clear precisely what events Mark 13 is talking about. But what is sure is that the God who nurtured this world into existence has not abandoned us, nor ever will.

Imagining the text

John the Baptizer appeared in the wilderness, proclaiming a baptism of repentance . . . And people from the whole Judean countryside and all the people from Jerusalem were going out to him, and were baptized by him in the river Jordan, confessing their sins. (Mark 1.4–5)

In reflecting on the ministry of John the Baptist as he is portrayed in Mark's Gospel – see 1.2–8 (Advent 2), and also 6.14–29 (Proper 10) – this poem imagines what the people of Jerusalem might have made of him. In many ways John is a typical prophetic figure, calling individuals and society to renewal – confrontational, disturbing, challenging, unconventional. But he also points beyond himself to another figure who is yet to come, who will bring in a new way of being and a different kind of encounter with God – a figure who is longed for, yet also feared.

The citizens of Jerusalem wonder about John the Baptist

Coming out of nowhere
With his crazy hair, freakish clothes,
He has the appearance of a deviant.

He is a kind of divine acrobat,
An enthusiast, agonized,
Well fed on the special diet of whatever circumstances allow –
Crunching the acrid shells of national disaster,
Tonguing the rare sweetnesses of consolation hidden from
  the rest of us –
Wild,
He is made strong,
And with his sacred vigour
He performs the searing arts of a prophet.

His technique is to startle and confront.
All carefully positioned plans he throws in the air
To bring down a new order,
Plotting out in the debris
A path we had not designed for ourselves,
Laid in a different direction from our own choosing.

Kings are enthralled and repelled by him.
With him it will end in tears.

He is a disrupter, a distraction,
Luring us out from our city, out from security
To find ourselves suddenly off-schedule,
Called back, back by him to an ancient track
Via water and the wilderness,
Into an uncharted land of promise, of encounter
Which is not yet ours,
Drawn to a meeting with the stranger
We have longed for.

But none of this is quite as we predicted.
It is not him, though we have found him compelling.
He has mangled our certainties,
Twisted everything into a future we cannot control.
After him
We must wait for another, even more dangerous.
He leaves us
Watching for the fire that sets all things ablaze.

Reflecting on the text

In these reflections we look at two of the themes of Advent, waiting and hoping, and offer a reflection on each. The final section picks up the focus of the poem and these exciting opening paragraphs of Mark's Gospel as we consider the messenger but especially the message that draws us in and demands from us a response.

Waiting

The season of Advent, like no other season in the Church's year, leads us into a waiting mode of living. We overhear children at home and in school saying to each other, 'I can't wait for Christmas.' In their eyes we glimpse how children are caught up in the excitement of waiting. The experience of waiting is a common one and it shapes the rhythm of all our lives. We wait for trains, for the postman, or for pay day.

One of the influences on our own theological thinking and pastoral work is a book by a writer called Bill Vanstone. In *The Stature of Waiting* he describes Jesus as a waiting figure – as shown most clearly in the garden of Gethsemane.[1] Jesus discloses in that waiting – as he waits in exposure and helplessness for what is to come – the deepest dimension of the glory of God. When we think of Jesus, we think of him waiting, trusting, being open and vulnerable and exposed.

Although the experience of waiting is a common human experience, we have created a world within which waiting is undesirable. This shapes our financial culture. Do you remember the advert for the first credit card, 'Access takes the waiting out of wanting'? Our consumerist culture is keen to make us spend and to fund that spending with loans of money. Our grandparents rarely bought anything without waiting while they saved up the money for the purchase. We on the other hand live in a world where we are promised that we can have what we want, and have it now – and more than that, we can have now what we neither want nor need.

Jesus shows us that waiting has its own value and dignity. Advent is the invitation to wait with hope for the future that is to come. God's future is not an invitation we find easy to accept. We live in a time when thoughts of the future may fill people with fear – and not with hope and joy. We must learn to hope, to rest, to pray and to wait.

W. H. Auden expressed our Advent hope in this way:

---

[1] W. H. Vanstone, *The Stature of Waiting* (London: Darton, Longman & Todd, 1982).

Because of His visitation, we may no longer desire God as if He were lacking: our redemption is no longer a question of pursuit – but surrender to Him who is always and everywhere present. Therefore at every moment we pray that, following Him, we may depart from our anxiety into His peace.

Hope

We sometimes wonder whether it is easier to live with some meaning, however inappropriately constructed, than to live without any meaning or purpose at all. And certainly some meanings are better than others. Perhaps it is easier to say, 'There's always someone else worse off than me' than, 'Well, this is my lot and I'd better just get on with it.'

What kind of meaning do you live with and how do you share it with others? In what and for what do we hope? How do we live with our unanswered questions?

Perhaps these last decades will be characterized by historians and theologians as being a crisis of meaninglessness set against essential materialism and decadence. This materialism and decadence have given rise to some order and control but also to threat and chaos. There are more and more people living without hope. I think that this is a critical area of human experience where Christian women and men might be careful listeners and guides. Hopeless people turn to an increasingly alarming range of drugs to alleviate their pain of hopelessness.

Look at the world around you and what do you see? Visit retail parks scattered across the country and what kind of hope do you glimpse? In the north-east of England, on the edge of Gateshead and Newcastle, is the Metro Centre. Visitors there are greeted with the notice: 'Welcome to the Metro Centre: a way of life'. A way of life? What does that way of life give to us? In what should we trust? What are the limits to the satisfaction of our needs? Is there any end to the decadence of our consumerism?

The experience of the absence of meaning and hopelessness are one and the same. Hope is about the creation of meaning, its fresh onset and its coming. The season of Advent reminds us of Mark 13's major point, that whatever it might feel like now we are not abandoned. We have grounds for hope. But we must distinguish hope from two other phenomena.

First, hope has nothing in common with prediction or projection. It has no connection with futurology. Why do people look to the stars for hope? Prediction claims that the future is so determined by the past that we can work out how it will grow out of the past. But we ought to know by now how limited is the range of interesting things that can be strictly predicted. Think about economics and how the predictions of rival practitioners conflict. Hope has much more to do with the unpredictability of the historical process.

Second, hope has nothing in common with optimism, a cheap, over-the-counter drug for maintaining denial. Hope is not only compatible with, but actually requires, a courageous facing of our frailty, death and vulnerability. Hope is not having excuses for optimism. It is a strenuous expectation of creative newness and meaning in our lives. It is faith in the meaningfulness of our personal and common future. Hope gives meaning to the present by conveying meaning about our future. It can help us live by trust with the tentative, the confusing, the fearful bits of the jigsaw that won't be forced into the framework or picture.

The answer Mark's Gospel gives us is this. We proclaim that God is the being of all being, the life of all life, the source and fulfilment of all. By God we mean the one who transcends space and time. Our future is real in the one who is not confined within space and time, but is infinite.

The Gospel proclaims that God has created within time a means of a future – to seep into the present in order to change it in hope. For us this is given in the death, burial and resurrection of Christ. Hope is the irradiation of the present with the light of the future that is with and in God. The secret of Christian identity is that faith in Christ and his future, faith in the reality of our future in him, is immeasurably stronger than the determinations of the past. Human beings have found comfort in supposing themselves powerless victims of the capricious turns of fortune's wheel, or imagining themselves controlled by astral forces in the sky. Being a Christian is to protest against religious determinism or the piety of fatalism. Our true identity is to be found in God: he is our journey and our journey's end; our true end and fulfilment. To live in hope is to know that I am who I am becoming. Christ in me makes continual space for newness within me. Hope is potency, hope is strenuousness, hope is energy.

Yet hope is not romantic; it is what gives us energy when there is nothing human to go on. There is creation by God out of nothing. We are co-creators with God of a future in hope. We create out of nothing, when good outcomes cannot be expected, when there are no grounds for optimism, when, from the human point of view, our personal lives and the lives of our society seem certain to go to waste or to hell. Hope cannot be represented as grand or secure, only as something vulnerable, even fragile.

For us this hope is best glimpsed in those people who live openly for goodness; serving and responding to the goodness in others, especially when it seems well hidden. Hope is proclaimed when we seek to listen and understand rather than speak and judge. Hope is nurtured when we choose love over hate, peace over war; when we choose the gaps in our understanding and knowledge rather than the security of wanting always to be right. Hope can enlighten our world when we care amid the selfishness of complacency. In such ways we can make a difference – our world can be made beautiful for God and humanity.

The message and the messenger

During Advent we consider John the Baptist as an intriguing and challenging figure. Imagine him: sober, serious, telling the people to prepare – prepare, beware and repent. There are four elements in John's life and ministry that we might consider here: the messenger; the message; the proclamation of the message; and the heart of the message.

First, the messenger or the forerunner. John the Baptist, who went ahead with the message, 'Prepare the way, make a clear path, make ready – get ready – the Lord is coming!' Open up a highway to your heart and life that the King of Glory may come in – an inner preparation of heart and mind to prepare for God. The Lord God, the rightful King of all our lives, comes to lift up, not to condemn, but offering pardon. The forerunner invites us to get ready to welcome our Maker, the one who offers us life.

Second, the message. Life is beautiful, like the flowers of the field. But, like the flowers of the field, that beauty fades, withers and dies. Our human lifespan is short, but the seed of withered grass comes to life again, for it is buried deep in the ground. God holds all things in love and in this holding of death and life offers us the possibility of new life. We can move into new life. This life is on offer. Its sell-by date never passes.

Third, the proclamation of the message. Look around and see God's handiwork. Look within and see God's image; her mark stamped on you. Behold your God, look at Jesus – and discover the hidden depths of God. The invitation is to follow God on this journey of life; a challenge that reaches down the centuries to face each of us again today. Look at him. Follow him, for he has the words of life.

Fourth, the heart of the message. God reminds us that it is good news we declare. This God meets our deepest needs. He is a shepherd, gently leading. He feeds us and gathers us in his arms. He cares for us and loves us – yes, he loves – that over-used, under-valued and misunderstood, yet vital word.

The message is the same, even if it has to be phrased differently. People do not change – they still need loving and caring for. We all need the good news that life need not be purposeless and selfish, self-centred existence with passing pleasures. We all need a focus of worship, and our task is to be the forerunner proclaiming the love of God.

Action, conversation, questions, prayer

Action

Take an opportunity to express words of hope in a situation of relentless negativity or criticism.

Conversation and questions

- Are there times when you have felt abandoned as a person or as a community? What words or gestures have given you real comfort in times of trouble? Who are the prophetic figures (like John the Baptist) who challenge or disturb us?
- What do you enjoy about waiting? What do you find difficult?
- What do you most hope for?

Prayer

O Lord our God,
make us watchful and keep us faithful
as we await the coming of your Son our Lord;
that, when he shall appear,
he may not find us sleeping in sin
but active in his service
and joyful in his praise;
through Jesus Christ our Lord.
Amen. *Common Worship*

2

Christmas

Exploring the text

Mark's Gospel provides slim pickings at Christmas time. Unlike the Gospels of Matthew and Luke it provides no run-up to the birth of Jesus and no account of the events surrounding his birth. It does not even, like John's Gospel, provide a poetic introduction that summons our imaginations back to the dawning of time. Instead Mark catapults us into the start of Jesus' adult ministry with his baptism by John in the river Jordan. This means that Jesus' family is treated differently in Mark from the other Gospels.

Families in Mark

There is very little in Mark to give us a sense of Jesus' family. Mary is only named once – possibly twice – and at that obliquely. In Mark 6.3 Jesus is identified as a carpenter who was the son of Mary and the brother of James, Joses, Judas and Simon. In Mark 15.40 and 47 two women are described as watching the crucifixion. One of them is Mary Magdalene and another, also called Mary, is described as being the mother of James and Joses. It is striking that this Mary has two sons of the same name as Jesus' brothers, but these names were quite common in the Jewish world and it would be very odd to name the woman as the mother of James and Joses and not of Jesus in this context.

The only other time Mary appears in Mark's Gospel is early on in Jesus' ministry, in Mark 3. In this account, when Jesus' family hear of what he is doing they seek to restrain him (3.21) and presumably to take him back home. Mary appears here in the text unnamed alongside Jesus' brothers, but Jesus refuses even to see them. What he does is almost as shocking today as it was then. He declares that they are no longer his family, stating instead that those listening to his message are now his family: 'And looking at those who sat around him, he said, "Here are my mother and my brothers! Whoever does the will of God is my brother and sister and mother"' (3.34–35). Mark emphasizes the contrast by using the word 'outside' twice (in vv. 31 and 32) to refer to Jesus' own family, whereas those listening to him are described twice as those 'around him'. By doing this Mark emphasizes the new boundaries that are drawn in the kingdom so that even family members become outsiders and those who barely know Jesus but accept his message become insiders.

Jesus' almost brutal dismantling of the family is much starker in Mark's Gospel than it is in Matthew or Luke. In each of these the birth narratives and other references to Mary and Jesus' family act as a counterbalance to the harsher message of the new drawing of relationships in God's kingdom. Mark, however, has only this story, and as a result the unsettling message – that the kingdom takes apart nearly everything that we consider fixed – stands out much more strongly.

The unsettling kingdom

Jesus' willingness to redraw family boundaries and make relationships with those that would otherwise be outcasts in society reminds us both of the importance of the kingdom and of its cost. Although Mark's Gospel contains the phrase 'the kingdom of God' relatively infrequently (14 times in contrast to the 31 uses of 'kingdom of heaven' in Matthew), it is vitally important for the Gospel. Mark tells us that it is the first thing that Jesus proclaimed when he began his ministry: 'Now after John was arrested, Jesus came to Galilee, proclaiming the good news of

God, and saying, "The time is fulfilled, and the kingdom of God has come near; repent, and believe in the good news"' (1.14–15). And it appears again extensively at two key points in Jesus' ministry, in 4.1–34, where Jesus tells the parable of the sower, and in 10.14–25, in the discussion about entry into the kingdom. The kingdom of God is, therefore, the central pillar of Jesus' proclamation and teaching in Mark.

Important though it is, the kingdom of God is unsettling and surprising, perhaps even more so in Mark than in the other Gospels. Mark stresses that the kingdom of God is something that not everyone will understand: 'And he said to them, "To you has been given the secret of the kingdom of God, but for those outside, everything comes in parables"' (4.11). Indeed the irony is that in this verse Jesus is speaking to the disciples, to whom, he says, the secret of the kingdom of God has been given – but, as we noticed in the Introduction, in chapters 4—8 even they do not understand the nature of the kingdom.

So the kingdom is hard to comprehend. It is also mysterious, growing secretly – like a mustard seed – until suddenly it is discovered to be a full-grown tree. Some interpreters of the mustard seed parable (Mark 4) suggest that it might also be unwelcome. Mustard was invasive: wild mustard was a weed that infested planted crops and was hard to get rid of; domestic mustard was equally invasive even if deliberately planted. Mustard didn't grow very large: to call it a tree would be an exaggeration, but anything that attracted birds into the middle of a crop would be unwelcome indeed. In a similar way the kingdom attracts the unwelcome members of society, the outcasts with whom Jesus spent so much time.

The kingdom that Jesus proclaimed as being near is hard to comprehend and mysterious, but it is growing secretly and at some point will come with great power and will be easily visible by all. Mark 9.1 speaks clearly of a time when God's kingdom will be seen coming in power: 'And he said to them,

"Truly I tell you, there are some standing here who will not taste death until they see that the kingdom of God has come with power."' Just like Mark 13, this passage has caused extensive discussion. Jesus appears to be saying here that there are some people listening to him who will not die before they see the kingdom coming in power. Since the second coming has not yet happened, this raises the question of whether Jesus, or Mark, was wrong. Some scholars argue that is the case and that Jesus or Mark, or both, fully expected the second coming to happen very soon and were incorrect in that expectation. Others take a less controversial view. Some argue that the verse is about recognition and that Jesus' statement means that there are listeners standing before him who will be able to see and comprehend the entirety of the kingdom – and all it means – during their lifetime, whereas others will either not see it at all or will see it only in part. An even more prosaic explanation is that this saying occurs in the chapter in which Peter and James and John see Jesus transfigured on the mountain (9.2–8) and is in fact referring to that.

Just as with Mark 13, it is unlikely that we will be able to solve the question of when the kingdom of God will – or did – come with power, but what is clear is the nature of the kingdom. The kingdom of God or, as some scholars prefer to call it, God's kingship, is something that breaks into our world but which is hard to understand and is often unsettling and uncomfortable. The kingdom of God surprises us time and time again. It is never predictable, and is sometimes unwelcome. The kingdom completely dismantles the boundaries and relationships on which we rely so much. It demands that we think again about who our family and friends really are. It questions who is inside and who outside. It throws the doors wide open in welcome to all who recognize the kingdom, whoever they might be. The kingdom of God challenges us over and over again to look again at the world and see it differently.

Imagining the text

> Whoever does the will of God is my brother and sister and mother. (Mark 3.35)

The absence of any birth narrative in Mark gives us an opportunity to take a different approach from the usual seasonal conventions at Christmas, and to consider the radical nature of discipleship which Jesus teaches and practises in the Gospel.

The following fantasy dialogue between Oprah Winfrey and Mary the mother of Jesus explores the hints which Mark's Gospel gives of the strain in family relationships which arose as a result of Jesus' ministry (3.20–30, Proper 5; 6.1–6, Proper 9; 10.17–31, Proper 23). In articulating the struggle which she has come through, as a caring mother, to understand the costly and dangerous vocation of her son, Mary witnesses to God's grace at work in her: a model of faithful discipleship which wrestles to take hold of the truths of God's will and purpose even when they are obscure or unconventional, or even seem hurtful.

Oprah Winfrey gets to heaven for a special Christmas interview with the Blessed Virgin Mary

M Ah, Oprah . . . welcome, my dear, come in. Do sit down, make yourself at home. Have a satsuma.

O Thank you . . . thank you . . . um, I'm not sure what to call you . . . you have so many titles . . . Do I say, *Your Fullness of Grace*?

M [*Laughs*] It's not like you to be lost for words, Oprah . . . No titles today. Just call me Mary.

O Mary? Just Mary?

M That's right, just Mary.

O You are Mary the mother of Jesus, aren't you? There are a lot of women up here named Mary . . . it's Mary the mother of Jesus that I'm looking for – *the* Mary . . . Mary from Nazareth.

M Yes, that's me: Mary the mother of Jesus. Jesus is my eldest, my first-born child. I've been called all kinds of names because of him! But in my own mind I am always *Mary*. After all . . . I'm mother of other children too you know – his brothers . . . James, Joses, Judas, Simon – and then there are the girls, Jesus' sisters . . . though the sisters never quite get the attention that they should. Boys can hog the limelight sometimes, don't you think, Oprah?

O Speaking as a multi-billionaire celebrity, Mary, I must say I've never found that to be a problem! But I was wondering if you would become my mentor – there's no one on earth who's got your profile. You're special! You're famous! You're the most famous woman in history!

M Me?! . . . The most famous woman in history?! . . . Well, well, Oprah, that's quite a statement.

O But it's true, Mary. Just look at all these Yuletide celebrations . . . you're everywhere – Mary with her baby Jesus. You're on all the cards and packaging, your name in all the carols and hymns! And then there's the stained glass and the statues, the pictures and the manuscripts; every other church has your name attached, schools and colleges, street names, shrines . . . there are even islands and whole cities named after you. There are vast libraries full of books about you. How does it feel to be so significant, Mary, sitting there in the stable with the Christ-child, the woman at the centre of everyone's favourite celebration?

M Mmm . . . between ourselves, Oprah, I don't always feel that comfortable at Christmas.

O Really? Mary the mother of Jesus uncomfortable with Christmas? Gee . . . that's quite a scoop!

M Is that really so strange? It wasn't always easy, you know . . .

O: Oh, no . . . expecting before you were married, explaining it all to Joseph, your waters breaking whilst you were on a donkey, giving birth in a strange town and, oh, in such ghastly unhygienic surroundings; and then all those smelly animals and strange visitors crowding in on you . . . no, not easy at all, Mary. But it makes a great story! Someone like you, such a special lady, slumming it in Bethlehem! We just love the drama!

M Oh, those things . . . I'm not referring to all that, Oprah.

O No? Then what?

M It wasn't always easy living with *him*.

O With whom? Joseph? Surely he understood, got over it in time . . . God's plan and all that . . . ?

M No, no . . . Joseph was a darling . . . such a lovely strong man, such a good man . . .

O So who? Who wasn't easy, Mary?

M Jesus . . . It wasn't always easy living with Jesus.

[*Stunned silence*]

O Mary . . . *Honey* . . . tell me more . . .

M Well . . . he was fine as a baby, no trouble at all . . . the occasional rash and colic, sleepless nights . . . but on the whole he was a very contented child . . . And as a boy there's very little to say . . . I taught him his prayers, the psalms, the great stories of our tradition . . . he went to classes and to worship without any trouble – not like his cousin John, who was such a rebel, always wanting to do his own thing –

O Just stick to Jesus. Tell me about Jesus, Mary . . .

M Well, Jesus was genuinely such a good boy, a real son of a carpenter, learning the trade, such a feel for his wood and knowing all the different joints . . . He was a natural, so skilled, so deft and fast, from one job straight to the next, taking to the business like a hammer to a nail . . . And the piety, the piety was so . . . um, it was so beautiful . . . so attractive.

O Beautiful?

M Yes . . . beautiful, to see a young working man so close to God, so familiar with the prophets, so committed to our family and village and to the shop – that was so lovely. He could draw people to him, they wanted to come close, somehow he would make it all better for them, they would see things differently.

O So what's the problem, Mary?

M I'm sometimes sad at Christmas because it reminds me of what might have been . . . a wife for him, children, a comfortable home, loyal friends, people that cared. He could have stayed put, become a respected figure in our community, a leader for the people . . .

O So from your perspective, Mary, did it all go wrong with your eldest son? What happened? Did Jesus change?

M No, no, he didn't exactly change . . . in the light of all that happened later I would say now that Jesus became more himself . . . But at the time it was dreadful, such a shock . . . You see he just took off, started teaching beyond the village, giving all his time and energy to whoever came to him . . . Not family and friends, Oprah, but complete strangers . . . Mad people, some of them, and trouble-makers, religious obsessives trying to catch him out . . . and they never stopped coming, morning, noon and night they would come, hounding him with their questions and problems . . . I can see why they pursued him, these people who became his disciples and all those endless problem cases: he was compelling, exceptional, profound . . . Oh, he was such a wonderful teacher and healer, he set people free, he seemed to be able to solve all kinds of intractable mangled situations . . . I was proud of him, Oprah, I was proud to be his mother . . .

O Do I hear a 'but' in there somewhere, Mary?

M But . . . I couldn't cope with the way our Jesus became . . . I couldn't cope, nor the other children. You see, Oprah, he abandoned us and threw away everything we stood for . . . or that's how it felt at the time.

O Abandoned you? What do you mean?

M Jesus gave up the carpentry, and he seemed to turn his back on all that had been so important before. He left the brothers and sisters who relied on him, he never came home, wouldn't eat, wouldn't sleep, wouldn't stand still for a moment . . . we began to think he was ill, out of his mind, fanatical . . . I was so worried that he would do damage to himself, wear himself out, get himself in trouble with the strange enchanting stories he began to tell about God. We were beside ourselves.

O Oh, Mary, I never realized it was like this for you . . .

M No, most people don't see it . . . how difficult it was for a mother to have him surrounded by others, keeping family out, confusing us with all the contradictory things we heard him teach – one minute reminding us to honour father and mother, and then the next breath he was on about leaving behind inheritance and family for the sake of God's kingdom. Some people thought he was marvellous of course, but me and the children, we felt outside it all, excluded. People would ask, 'Where did *he* get ideas like this?' as if our Jesus was a nobody! It was so hurtful to hear all those things at the time, before we came to understand.

O And what was it that you came to understand, Mary?

M That my son Jesus was Wisdom's child.

O I don't follow you.

M I came to understand that Jesus had a project, a particular 'job' as we would say in the carpenter's shop. And the job was to be God's presence among us – God's healing and freedom and wisdom and peace – all freely available to us, and that to be the way he was he had to give the whole of himself, not just a part.

O So are you saying, as a disappointed mother you came to accept the way your son turned out?

M What happened to Jesus broke my heart: the betrayal, the torture, the cross. I had to let him go through all that; the whole family had to let him be who he was meant to be in God's plan.

O So, Mary, is Christmas a time full of regret for you, as the mother of a baby who would grow up to be as much misunderstood as admired?

M No one should imagine, when they see me holding Jesus as a baby, that it was an easy thing for me to be his mother. My child grew up into a man nailed to a cross. Looking at that sweet child no one should fool themselves that it was an easy thing for my son to be Jesus. My Jesus gave his whole self to be God among us.

O So you know from your own experience what hard times some families go through, Mary?

M It's not easy to accept one another when our expectations are shattered. I know how painful it can be to let those closest to you be the people God intends them to be. But that's the price of really loving another person. I learnt that my child is also God's child, and that to be both is life's fulfilment for each and all of us.

Reflecting on the text

How real is Christmas for us? In this section we offer two reflections. The first explores the celebration of Christmas in a place that can shatter the most secure of us – a place of fear, paradox and uncertainty: literally of life and death. These are human experiences that are sometimes hard to comprehend even for those of us who are trained to care.

In the absence of any Christmas narrative we invite you to consider what image of Christmas you would choose to sum up the surprise of the kingdom breaking in to open up our hearts and minds.

Christmas in hospital

It's the afternoon of Christmas Eve and as the hospital chaplain I am busy visiting patients. Some are in bed; many sit by their beds, full of expectation, with a variety of carrier bags surrounding them. Conversation inevitably focuses on where they will be tomorrow. Expressions of relief at going home (at last) coupled with real sadness at staying: 'I overheard a nurse saying that it's only the really sick who stay,' shares one woman, which feeds her own and others' anxieties. Amid all this is frenetic activity: discharge notes, doctors looking at test results, Sister managing to get through her jobs. There are parties in wards and departments: some love Christmas, others loathe it. I catch up with various people, am touched by offers of Christmas lunch and enjoy dipping into the numerous boxes of chocolates and mince pies.

After opening some Christmas cards I join my Catholic friends for their Mass, the first Mass of Christmas. I look at the burning candles and the expectation in the eyes of the children. Then we gather together for our round of carol singing. Consultants and nurses, the chaplaincy team and lots of noisy children. Lights are dimmed and the carols are sung around each ward. Most know the words by heart and tears are shed, hands held; some turn away, more interested in the TV set. I wonder, what does this mean to them all?

After some refreshment at a colleague's home I travel across the city to a midnight service. I join the congregation to worship, to be fed and to pray for our chaplaincy work in the hospital. The city roads are empty and it's straight to bed for an early start tomorrow.

I greet the night staff and turn down an early morning sherry in the Night Sister's office. It has been a quiet night. On my way to the admissions unit I meet a tearful man whose wife died here three years ago. He seems confused, paralysed by his loss. I offer to take him home and he accepts. It's hard to hide my surprise at his house, empty, and at the table set for two. 'I always set her place . . . I do miss her.' I make him some tea and then leave, aware of his loneliness, especially acute today. Back in the hospital the team are gathering for morning worship. The porters help transport our congregation and the worship is simple and moving.

For some there are tears and I can't help but wonder if this will be their last Christmas. A Muslim joins us and sits attentively in the corner. We chat after the service and he asks why every person in the hospital isn't in chapel. I muse with him about religion and belief in the modern world and ask him what he thinks should be done. 'I want to know,' he replies sharply, 'what all those people will say to God when they meet him after they die.' Ward Communions follow, and more visits. There are very few patients around. They are sick. Some are dying and all are away from home. I feel a small part of their sadness and vulnerability, see their tears. There is music, noise and laughter. The staff wear tinsel, decorations abound and they want to have a nice time. Yet underneath all this is a kind of loneliness. Some of the staff too are far from home, while others have opted to work today for a variety of reasons.

How does one make creative and redemptive sense of this? In my visiting and conversation I feel a deep sense of stark contrasts, of paradox and dissonance. Birth and death, the old and young, the sick and healthy, joy and faith, hope and despair, pain and vulnerability, expressed in many ways, somehow all belong together. The parallels and connections are yours to make. It's been a busy day. I retire to friends who have the energy to cook a turkey and relax. I feel the tiredness of the day and my mind is full of a range of images. Merry Christmas?!

Images of Christmas

When I was a boy in the north-east of England I had a paper round. The lead-up to Christmas was a time of great anticipation and excitement. People used to leave Christmas boxes in envelopes stuck into the letterbox. Usually they would contain 50p but occasionally a pound note (do any of you remember those?), and several delightful *Daily Telegraph* readers always gave me a five-pound note! I remember one year I collected nearly £25. It was a lot of money in those days, a sum that amazed and delighted me (and still does). Sometimes we need to look and feel with the eyes and heart of a child.

With the size of modern newspapers my old paper round would be impossible: the weight of papers would be too great to carry and they would be too voluminous to fit into the bag. At Christmas time we are offered many images and narratives. Every year there are a greater variety of Christmas cards, attempting to offer a personal expression of the meaning of the season. One year I was intrigued to see what various celebrities had chosen to go on the front of their Christmas cards. Some chose photographs of themselves – the Blairs playing happy families in the front of 10 Downing Street; the Archbishop with his grandchildren. Someone chose to picture their animals, and another had a digitally represented engagement ring (which we were told cost a mere $400,000).

These images are the ephemera of our media-spinning modern life. Are we living in reality, or in a virtual reality invented for us by spin-doctors? But there were other, more demanding images – images that forced you to take them seriously, whether you wanted to or not. A child dying on the streets of India being comforted by a nun. For another card a fashion designer chose a picture of an Afghan woman weeping, her grief and agony palpable.

So here are two ways of looking at life, and two ways of looking at Christmas. The first is tinselled nostalgia for a glittery past, a fantasy that winter only looks cold but is really glowingly warm, accompanied by synthesized Christmas carol tunes, the words mostly forgotten and very likely not understood. We want to escape. We need to fantasize. Religion can collude with this.

A different picture is offered in Mark's Gospel. The kingdom of God surprises us. It is never predictable. The kingdom completely dismantles the boundaries and relationships on which we rely so much. It demands that we think again about who our family and friends really are. The kingdom of God challenges us over and over to look again at the world and see it differently.

The peace and goodwill that the kingdom proclaims, the reconciliation and love that Mark will explore, are perhaps achieved by facing up to the paradoxical realities of how we mark Christmas and which of its symbols are meaningful for us. This spiritual work of reflection must include some of the uncomfortable realities about ourselves and in what we trust.

The work of the engraver Eric Gill is rich and evocative. On one of his Christmas cards he puts at the centre a simple representation of the nativity. But in the far left-hand corner he depicts a cross in the form of a gallows. In this representation, Christ's birth and death are placed side by side. 'The holly bears a prickle, as sharp as any thorn' – as sharp as any thorn in the crown of thorns. It is a sweet picture of a mother adoring her child – and a picture of the sacrifice he will make for love. The child will give his whole life for the world. Here is a Christmas that is uncomfortable and unsettling.

Action, conversation, questions, prayer

Action

Over the Christmas period, get in touch with someone who you know will find the season hard.

Conversation and questions

- Are there life choices that others have made which you find difficult to understand or appreciate?
- What images sum up the meaning of the Christmas message for you?
- When Christmas comes, what are the most challenging aspects of enjoying and appreciating the festival?

Prayer

Loving word of God,
you have shown us the fullness of your glory,
in taking human flesh.
Fill us, our bodily life,
with your grace and truth;
that our pleasure may be boundless,
and our integrity complete,
in your name.
Amen — Janet Morley

3

Epiphany

Exploring the text

In the season of Epiphany we celebrate the revelation of God in the world, and in particular his revelation to the Magi in Matthew's Gospel. Yet again this idea seems to run counter to Mark's Gospel, which appears on the surface to be more concerned with secrecy than with revelation. If we look closer, however, it becomes clear that the whole of the Gospel is concerned with the intertwined themes of secrecy and revelation.

Secrets and revelations

One of the oddest features of Mark's Gospel is the lengths that Jesus appears to go to in order to keep himself and his identity secret. When we look at the kingdom of God, one feature that jumps out is the fact that for some people the kingdom of God will remain in 'parables', which seems to mean it will remain oblique, unclear and hard to comprehend. It is easy to rationalize this as referring to people who, for whatever reason, simply cannot grasp the message that Jesus came to bring. Mark's Gospel, however, seems to suggest that it is something more than this. At various points throughout the Gospel Jesus seems to go out of his way to prevent people either from understanding his message or from proclaiming it. So in Mark 4.11–12 Jesus says: 'To you has been given the secret of the kingdom of God, but for those outside, everything comes in parables; in order that "they may indeed look, but not perceive, and may indeed listen, but not understand; so that they may not turn again and be forgiven."' In addition, four times during his ministry Jesus commands the person he has just healed not to tell anyone (1.43–44; 5.43; 7.36; 8.26) and he forbids the demons he is casting out from saying that they recognize him (1.25, 34; 3.12).

Some interpreters have called this the Messianic Secret and have seen this motif of secrecy as lying at the heart of Mark's Gospel. Others would argue that this is overstating the secrecy motif in Mark. Jesus does indeed forbid people four times to tell others that he has healed them and three times reprimands demons, but at other points in the Gospel he seems to be quite happy for people to notice him and to observe his miracles. So, for example, in the account of the healing of the man from Gerasa who was possessed by demons (Mark 5.1–20), Jesus explicitly tells the man to 'Go home to your friends, and tell them how much the Lord has done for you, and what mercy he has shown you' (v. 19). Of course this may have been possible because the man lived outside Galilee and Judea, but it does demonstrate that secrecy is not a consistent strand in Mark's Gospel.

Three moments of revelation

Indeed there are moments when revelation is as important as secrecy, if not more important. At three key moments in Mark's Gospel Jesus is declared to be the Son of God. These three key moments fall evenly throughout the Gospel. The first occurs at Jesus' baptism by John (1.2–11). When Jesus comes up out of the water, Mark describes the heavens being torn apart and the Spirit descending on Jesus like a dove and a voice coming from heaven which declares Jesus to be God's beloved Son with whom he is well pleased. A similar event happens halfway through Mark's Gospel, when Jesus is transfigured. In Mark 9.2–10, Jesus takes Peter, James and John to the top of a mountain. On this occasion Jesus is transfigured so that his clothes dazzle and a cloud covers them. Again they hear a voice coming from the cloud declaring that Jesus is God's beloved Son and that they should listen to him.

These two events are significant. In the Old Testament, one of the signals of the presence of God was some form of natural phenomenon like the opening of heaven: wind, rain, lightning, hail, thunder or cloud. Another signal of God's presence was hearing the voice of God. These events are often called 'theophanies' or appearances of God and we find them at regular intervals throughout the Old Testament (such as with Moses on Mount Sinai, or Elijah on Mount Carmel). Mark's telling of these accounts seems to place them directly in the category of theophany.

The third of the three revelations in Mark's Gospel is slightly different, but importantly so. It occurs when Jesus is on the cross. As he approaches his death darkness falls over the land, and when he dies the veil in the temple is torn in two (15.33, 38). The importance of this was that the veil of the temple was what separated the Holy of Holies from the rest of the temple. The Holy of Holies was the place where God dwelt and the veil was in place to protect the priests, who might be in the temple serving God, from seeing God and perishing. The tearing in two of the temple veil, then, was similar in importance to heaven being torn apart at Jesus' baptism: that which had until then been kept secret was now revealed. As the veil is torn apart, in Mark, we hear a voice declaring that Jesus is God's Son – as on both the previous occasions. The difference this time, however, is that the voice does not belong to God. This time the voice belongs to a centurion whose role it was to crucify Jesus. For the first time in Mark's Gospel, a human being – and a Roman soldier at that – has taken on the role of God and announced the identity of Jesus to the world.

Some people have suggested that the centurion did not say that Jesus was 'the Son of God', merely that he said that he was 'a Son of God'. The problem with this is that it is not always necessary to include the word 'the' in Greek where we would need it in English. The words of the centurion could mean either 'a Son of God' or 'the Son of God'. We simply do not and cannot know which the centurion meant here. It seems likely, however, that Mark intends us to read this exclamation alongside that of God at Jesus' baptism and transfiguration. Given this, Mark probably intends his readers to hear 'the Son', not 'a Son', here.

Proclamation of Jesus' identity

Mark's Gospel finely balances secrecy with revelation, hiddenness with openness. It is important to recognize that these two themes fit together like opposite sides of the same coin. Mark does not include one or the other but both. A key to understanding this double theme in Mark seems to be offered by the story of Jesus' healing of the blind man from Bethsaida (8.22–26). When Jesus first heals the man, he sees people 'like trees, walking'; Jesus then lays his hands over his eyes again and then he sees well. Peter in Caesarea Philippi, immediately after this healing, has a similar experience (8.27–33). When Jesus asks who they think he is, Peter declares that Jesus is the Messiah, but he becomes distressed when Jesus tells them that this will involve suffering and death. Peter, just like the blind man in Bethsaida, has partial sight and can see some but not all of who Jesus was. The great danger Jesus faced in his ministry was that people would proclaim the half truth of what they had seen rather than the whole truth of who he was. Jesus spoke in parables so that people had to work at understanding him. He wanted them to take their time, put all the pieces of the jigsaw together and understand him in his entirety before proclaiming who he was. Again we are brought back to the parable of the mustard seed. The seed takes its time to grow, but once grown makes a great impact on its environment.

The theme of secrecy and revelation in Mark's Gospel seems to have a similar thrust. The followers of Jesus had to take their time encountering Jesus in all his fullness. They might otherwise have jumped to the wrong conclusion and assumed that Jesus, Son of God, had come with military might to drive out the Romans. Indeed it took a Roman who watched Jesus' death to put the pieces together and work out who he really was. It is interesting that after his death and resurrection the women at the tomb are explicitly commanded to 'go, tell' (Mark 16.7). They now have all the pieces of the puzzle. They have seen Jesus' ministry, seen him die and now know that he is risen. They should now be able to look *and* perceive, listen *and* understand, turn *and* be forgiven. At the end of Mark's Gospel all the pieces are available, secrecy is no longer necessary. The women are invited to put the pieces together and to proclaim what they know. The way in which Mark's Gospel is written means that this challenge remains for us, as much as it did for the earliest disciples. We have all the pieces of the jigsaw; the question for us is what we intend to do with them.

Imagining the text

The following poem celebrates Jesus at his baptism in the river Jordan (Mark 1.4–11), when the voice from heaven proclaims, 'You are my Son, the Beloved; with you I am well pleased', thus echoing the expressed delight of the Creator God at the birth of the world he has made, and particularly at humankind made in his image (Gen. 1.26–31). Here in the poem the same creation, in the form of water, rejoices at the coming of God's Saviour: for in Jesus God will restore the fallen, polluted and degraded world to its true dignity and harmony. The response of the river in the poem anticipates the nature miracles which follow in the Gospel, where wind and waves acknowledge the authority of Jesus as the Christ of God (Mark 4.35–41, Proper 7; 6.45–51), bringing order and peace out of chaos as at the first creation (Gen. 1.1–5, Epiphany 1).

> What ails you, O sea, that you fled?
> O Jordan, that you turned back? (Psalm 114.5, NKJV)

Jesus is baptized in the river Jordan: water responds on behalf of all creation

When he stepped into me, it was then I became pure.

Though I had washed a million stinking garments,
carrying away in my flow
rain after rain
the stain of your industry and ablution,
your bleaching and dyeing and tanning –
not to mention the defecation of cities and sheep;

Though I have rinsed the skin of lepers clean,
flushed disease
and the blood of your wars
downstream,
out through my veins
with the elemental force that was mine since the Flood;

Though I perform all these miracles of cleansing for you,
you children of Eve and Adam,
dreamers of clear streams in the well-watered garden,
children of Moses, who turned Egyptian rivers to run with blood
and conjured seas to step aside for your escape;
though you hanker after purity and freedom
all your pollutions I have had to hold . . .

It was not until his calloused feet were planted on my
  smoothed-stone bed,
when I made my cold embrace of his calves (a walker's legs
  he had),
and played my swift dart in and out of the thighs
to see if I could topple him –
it was not until John swelled him down into me
with the long pour and the plunge . . .

only then I flowed freely

free as I did when the dove first drew me
out of deep dark chaos,
and now every sweet drop of me
standing in stone jars and welling up in fonts
tastes of the finest wine

newly infused as I am
with the life-force
for which all living things have waited.

Reflecting on the text

In the following two pieces we pick up a couple of important themes. The first piece deals with vulnerability – both ours and God's. We see the unfolding nature of God revealed in secrets and revelations and we ask, what kind of God might we trust?

The second is a letter of encouragement to Christians on their journey of faith.

On being vulnerable

This season of Epiphany is so easily overlooked, rich as it is in symbol and promise. Mark will continue to explore who Jesus is – mystery and revelation will be key themes for us to wrestle with on our journey.

The majesty and promise of Jesus has also to embrace the vulnerability which begins at birth and will end on the cross. Jesus arrived in the world naked and helpless as the rest of us, but, unlike the rest of us, he remained without defences for the whole of his life. As all of us grow older we learn to defend ourselves, putting up all kinds of devices that protect us, and distance ourselves from anything that might threaten us. Being exposed is a risky business; struggling to be ourselves in human relations is an activity within which we court disappointment and injury. No surprise that we engage in such relations with elaborate caution, taking care that we are not too often misunderstood. In being human we limit who we are vulnerable with; being trustful is hard work and for some almost impossible, as the fear of squandering intimacy feels a step too fraught with risk. The family, those who will not challenge us, our own circle or class, become the comfort zone beyond which we do not wish to squander that intimacy.

The danger in this is that gradually we love less and less; that, entrenched behind our own ramparts, we become more and more lonely, attempting to console ourselves with the familiar placebos of possessions, work or status.

Mark's Jesus offers us a vulnerable openness both to people and circumstances. In doing so he challenges us, exposes us to some fundamental truths about the way to live fully and freely. To deny this openness can be to slip into cynicism and even despair. It is too easy to close in on ourselves, reacting censoriously towards new ideas and being defensive to criticism. In feeling under attack we may attempt to secure our ground by making others feel guilty and afraid.

Vulnerability is a fact of our condition and should be accepted as a part of all our lives. We believe that God governs all things in heaven and on earth. If this is so, can the stupidities, cruelties and envies of our life be described as the work of Almighty God?

Affirming the rule of God in the world as we know it means coming to terms with the challenges and problems of life as it is. It means trusting and having faith in Jesus and his way as a key to understanding how we embrace the whole of our living. The key for us is Christ. The man born to be king is the crucial revelation of truth, and offers us a firm foundation of hope. As we journey through Mark we shall discover more of this Jesus and his meaning for us. There is no doubt-free faith – that is to say that life remains vulnerable, as love remains vulnerable. That is not weakness but its nature, and we cannot have it otherwise.

The God we affirm as the one who governs all things means that we cannot manipulate God to suit our comfort: it means the vulnerable God, the God who governs through and not in spite of vulnerability, the Father of whom Christ was the Son. And it is this that makes the difference. It makes the difference in how we understand who God is, his style of government, the importance that he attaches to human freedom, and within that freedom the possibility and certainty that things will go wrong.

This vulnerability, despite its perplexities, is the mainspring of our faith and hope.

An Epiphany letter of encouragement

Together we have been exploring discipleship – what God might want of us on our journey. When Christians eat together, pray together and break open God's word, transforming things can happen. In a Church preoccupied with disagreement and decline I've been so heartened by it. Most of you – not all, I think – have decided to commit yourselves to be disciples of Christ: to live the way, the journey, and travel with him. In my experience, the road is unlike any other that can be experienced or imagined – and it has brought, for me, a life full of treasures that I could never have dreamed of when I set out from the small village in County Durham where I was born and grew up.

From here on in you won't be more virtuous than ever you were. No new sanctity or wisdom or power is suddenly going to descend. Nonetheless, most of you know that you are the declared representatives of either the world's oldest and most persistent and superannuated superstition or the world's wildest and most improbable dream – or of the holy, living truth itself.

In unexpected places and at unexpected times, people of all sorts and conditions, believers and unbelievers, will make their way to you looking for something that often they can't name – any more than you can name it to them. Often their lives will touch yours when they are at their most vulnerable – when some great grief or gladness has swept away the barriers we erect between us – and you will be stripped naked by their nakedness.

Strange things will happen. Christ is present in places you'd never look for him in a thousand years. The great preacher, the fine music, the exquisite natural beauty might leave you cold – but the child in the doorway, the half-remembered dream, can speak of him and for him, with an eloquence that turns your knees to water.

You come to places where many paths meet – as all our paths have met briefly here, we friends who are strangers, we strangers who are friends. Much may come of these encounters but remember that it is the gift of lead, rather than that of gold, that often contains the treasure. And the person who seems to have least to offer turns out to have the most.

Whither then? Whither now, we cannot say. But the road goes on anyway. And we must follow if we can because it is our road, it is this road, it is the only road that matters.

I went to a theological college whose motto was 'Faithful is he who calls, who also will do it'. We need to trust and hope in the one who is faithful, the one who will never let us go.

I do not know what pitfalls lie ahead. You know that the world is full of dark shadows, to be sure; both the world without and the world within. And the road we are all set out on is long and hard – hard, often, even to find. But the word is trust. Trust the deepest intuitions of your heart. Trust the source of your own truest gladness. Turn this way and that, and never move; and so achieve that blessed stillness which is at the heart of all things. Trust the road. Above all else, trust him.

May God bless us on our journey into the future.

Action, conversation, questions, prayer

Action

Light a candle and sit for a while watching its flame.

Conversation and questions

- At what moments in your life have you felt that you have seen something of God? What did you feel like at these moments?
- How easy do you find being open or vulnerable with others?
- What encourages you most in your Christian journey?

Suggestions for prayer

- Pray for clarity of vision to see more of God.
- Pray for courage to be more vulnerable with those you love.
- Pray for encouragement on your Christian journey and that you might bring encouragement to others.

Prayer

Lord Jesus,
may your light shine on our way,
as once it guided the steps of the magi:
that we too may be led into your presence

and worship you,
the Child of Mary,
the Word of the Father,
the King of nations,
the Saviour of mankind;
to whom be glory for ever.
Amen. Frank Colquhoun

4

Lent

Exploring the text

During Lent we prepare ourselves for the Passion of Christ, looking forward to that time when Jesus' suffering and death will bring redemption to the world. In Mark's Gospel, we discover that we are not the only ones expecting Jesus' death: Jesus too looks forward to the time when he will suffer and die. In fact such occasions are so important in Mark's Gospel that many scholars believe that in these sayings we can discover something crucial about who Jesus thought he was.

The suffering of the Son of Man

In Mark's Gospel, as in the other Gospels, different titles are used of Jesus. The three most important in Mark are 'Son of God', 'Son of Man' and 'Messiah' or 'Christ' (Christ is simply the Greek translation of the Hebrew word Messiah). Of these titles 'Messiah' is the easiest to understand. It means in Hebrew 'anointed one' and refers first of all to anyone anointed to act on God's behalf, in the way that in the Old Testament certain priests, kings and prophets were anointed to do the task to which God called them. As time went on, however, the title seems to have been used by some people to refer to the hope that God would send someone in the future to save them from oppression. This title became so closely associated with Jesus that in the Gospels it is used almost as a part of his name: Jesus Christ.

The other two titles are far more complex to understand. On the surface they look straightforward: 'Son of Man' seems to refer to Jesus' humanity and 'Son of God' to his divinity. The problem is that they are not always used like this in the Gospels. 'Son of God' is the easier of the two. In Mark the title is only used three times (1.1; 3.11; 5.7) in that form, though as we noticed in the previous chapter, God refers to Jesus twice as his 'beloved Son' and the centurion at Jesus' death calls him the 'Son of God', translated by the NRSV as 'God's Son'. The phrase 'Son of God' was often used in the Old Testament to refer to the king (e.g. 2 Samuel 7.14) and this has raised the question of what it means when it is used of Jesus. Some scholars think that it simply refers to Jesus' role in God's kingdom and so implies Jesus' kingship; others would argue that it has a greater and more significant meaning than this and implies divinity.

The title 'Son of Man' has caused the most discussion of all, and scholars are far from agreed about what it might mean. It is the one title that Jesus uses of himself (all the others are used by other people of or to him) – and particularly in the context of what will happen to him in his death and resurrection. Some people have therefore argued that when he uses it, it is merely a weighty way of saying 'I'. Others argue that it has more theological significance than that. In the Old Testament, 'Son of Man' is used to describe human beings (e.g. Num. 23.19: 'God is not a human being, that he should lie, or a mortal [son of man], that he should change his mind'). In Daniel 7.13–14, the phrase is used to describe the one who would go to the Ancient of Days 'with the clouds' and who then received 'dominion and glory and kingship'. Although in the passage itself, logic demands that the Son of Man is a human being who receives from God reward on behalf of God's people, subsequent interpretation of it in Jewish literature (e.g. *1 Enoch*) ascribes to the Son of Man a future quasi-divine messianic role which is pre-eminent before God. Scholars cannot agree over whether, when Jesus used the title of himself, he used it simply to mean 'I'; to refer to this future messianic expectation; or to a mixture of the two.

Who did Jesus think he was?

One of the central questions that has exercised New Testament scholars over the years is who Jesus himself thought he was and, alongside that, who the Gospel writers thought he was. The question centres on the matter of whether either Jesus or the Gospel writers thought he was divine. For much of the twentieth century, the discussion about who Jesus was seen to be focused on the titles used by him of himself and about him by others. Although these titles remain significant, scholars recognize increasingly that we cannot understand everything about who Jesus was from the titles – and in particular from the history of how those titles were used in the period before Jesus. Leander Keck evocatively states, 'To reconstruct the history of titles as if this were the study of Christology is like trying to understand the windows of Chartres cathedral by studying the history of coloured glass.'[1] As a result attention is now focused on how the story told by Mark reveals to the reader who Jesus is: a Jesus who calls disciples; who heals the sick; who drives out demons; who controls the waters of chaos; and who understands his calling to be something that involves suffering, death and resurrection.

The suffering Son of Man

One of the striking, and significant, features of Jesus' use of the title 'Son of Man' in Mark's Gospel is that it often occurs in prophecies about his future suffering and death (8.31; 9.12, 31; 10.33, 45). These prophecies occur in the third section of Mark (8.27—10.52) when the Gospel's attention turns to the

---

[1] L. Keck, 'Toward the Renewal of New Testament Christology', *New Testament Studies* 32 (1986), pp. 362–77.

way of the cross. Whatever the background of the Son of Man sayings, the prophecies of Jesus' suffering and death add an additional element to Daniel's vision of the Son of Man receiving 'dominion and glory and kingship'. Jesus makes it very clear in these prophecies that the 'dominion and glory and kingship' that he, as the Son of Man, will receive, will involve suffering as well as triumph and death as well as victory. All the way through Mark's Gospel, Jesus makes clear that God's kingdom is not what we expect it to be; nor in fact is Jesus. He is not to be found among the rich and successful but among the poor and outcasts from society; not in the centre but on the margins; not at the heart of religion but among those whom religion shuns. Even the dominion and glory and kingship which he will receive is turned on its head, since he receives it on the cross. It is a dominion which is found in the giving up of his rights; a glory which is embraced fully in suffering; and a kingship which is enthroned on the cross. Jesus' prophecies do draw on Daniel's prophecy but, as so often in Jesus' life, in ways that people could not anticipate or expect.

During Lent, we prepare ourselves for the celebrations of Holy Week and Easter by reminding ourselves of who Jesus really was. The Son of Man prophecies are a good way into this. Throughout the Gospels Jesus defies all expectations of who he would be and calls us to look for him, now as then, in the places we least expect him to be.

Imagining the text

After his baptism and the descending of the Holy Spirit, Jesus is driven by that same Spirit into the wilderness for forty days, to be tempted by Satan. Mark's is the only Gospel to add 'and he was with the wild beasts' (1.13, Lent 1). Alone in the desert with these creatures but no human company, angels minister to him.

The next piece plays on the significance of the wild beasts and the angels for the identity and mission of Jesus as he sojourns in the wilderness. The reflection on the wild beasts takes the ancient form of an imagined bestiary in which creatures are ascribed a moral character or representative role; in this sense they are 'psychological beasts' as well as living creatures, indicating the human vulnerability of Jesus, subject as he is to the physical forces of nature and simultaneously to the inner struggles of isolation, displacement and doubt. Some creatures are threatening, some delightful: they all gather around Jesus as the new Adam, the one come to restore creation to its original God-intended harmony (see Gen. 1.1—2.3).

The ministering angels are interpreted here as personifications of the spiritual consolation that strengthens God's anointed in his trials, as the messengers of divine presence, guidance and support in times of trouble and spiritual agony, drawn from the experience of the people of Israel and of the prophets and patriarchs in the desert. They have the character of the five senses: sight, taste, smell, hearing, touch.

A Lenten bestiary in the company of angels

The first wild beast, first angel

The wild dove sings to comfort a solitary figure

Not all is alien here in the desert.
Yes, there are the harsher birds with their appetite for dead
  things,
Keeping open a constant eye for carrion or prey.
But there are those of us, hiding in the clefts of the rocks,
  who sing,

Keeping one another company year after year.
Remember it was one such as I
Who found the evidence for an end to animosity,
Flying over miles of watery waste
To gladden Noah's heart
As I will gladden yours
If only you will listen, morning and evening
To my quiet song
As it puts forth gently, like an olive branch,
Sound of the whole cosmos sounding out in praise.

The sight of the rainbow angel of the Covenant painting the sky

Displaying my stock of ochres and azures
I daub down the steep bank of sky
Colouring the bond between earth and heaven
Which the Maker of all things has set for a sign.

Look, look, I cry to those who are hurting,
To those who are bitter, or worn-down, or sad;
See what delight the Lord has for his creatures,
Look to the rainbow to know how things are.

The second wild beast, second angel

The hyena's insatiable hunger

We have circled you in a recurring little dance of death
Which sends us scuttling, sniffing, savouring the hours
Of your inevitable decline, your sizzling need –
O man without food, without water.

We are always hungry, starving
However much we eat,

However much we gorge ourselves
There is never enough inside us.

We are insatiable, unpleasable,
And we shall eat you again and again
As you feed away on yourself,
Feasting deep in the guts on your own regret,
Your guilt, your anxiety, your turmoil of confusion.
Your lack of resolution is our nourishment.

The taste of the angel of exceeding fruitfulness

I am the angel of exceeding fruitfulness.
My service is to sing God praises in difficult places,
To celebrate unlikely beginnings and treasure the impossible promises:
For God continues to bring out of nothing
New worlds unlike any other.
This truth I feast upon.
I invite many guests.

Though you may be hungry now with anger or regret,
Yearning for unattainable reassurances,
I will teach you what is sufficient,
I will show you the secrets of daily bread:
I will lead you to the place of Manna and quail,
Guide your struggle through hard rocks
To a springing well.

The third wild beast, third angel

The angry black dogs of depression and disillusionment

The last thing we expected
Was for you to befriend us.

We tracked you for days at a distance,
Lurking behind,
Threatening, growling,
Needing you to fear us,
To deny to yourself that we were there.

But you called us down, you named us, stroked us
like children,
Let us lie around you, calm.
With you there is no pretence, not even to self.
And the anger which fuels us,
This you acknowledge
And send bounding out to fetch back sticks
for you,
Turned into play.

The angel of sacrifice imparts the loving art of smell

Not the stench of cattle, sheep and doves
That the Father longs for now,
But the smell of the beloved,
Grasped firm, pulled close and held for ever,
That unmistakable scent
Of skin, the breath, the hair . . .
This is what he treasures.

The fourth wild beast, fourth angel

Poisonous sniping serpents

We watch you walking across the hills and plains of our
wilderness –
A trespasser.
We have been here for a thousand million years
And claim it as our habitat:

We preceded Moses,
We sniped at the ankles of the children of Israel
And we beset any pilgrim feet
With our special poison:
Feel our fangs swell you with distrust and impatience,
Sense our sour critique seep up your limbs
As you become too sore for any more travelling
And falling stagnant,
Comfortable yet uncomforted,
You succumb to our entropy
That is death for your soul.

Listen to the call of the angel of greeting

In the silence which seems like a void
You may hear me calling, calling:
I am the angel of greeting
And I sing open your soul
To the gladness of God
Who awaits you,
Who holds near his heart
The secret of your fulfilment and joy.

Come near as I whisper
All the fullness of God's love for you;
Take the music I will make for you,
Sing the song that is yours.

The fifth wild beast, fifth angel

Elephants, wolves, lions, flies

We see the human figure sitting hunched, alone.
We desire that you become the prey of envy, of isolation,
That you should long to hunt and hurt as we do:
For we are beasts of herd, of pack, of pride, of swarm,

We trample and devour;
We defend ourselves, we dominate each other,
We never deviate.
To us the loner is vulnerable, ailing,
And we shall tear him limb from limb
As he hates himself for having no one to lie next to him.

The touch of the angel who comforts the lonely

I am the angel of Solitude,
And I hold its precious ointment in my gentle hands.
My service is to soothe the inner ache of loneliness.
My balm will ease you,
Free you from the emptiness which grips you like a pain.
My fingers shall unleash you
To play in the astonishing presence of God,
I shall unbind you
To welcome the beauty of your own true self.

Reflecting on the text

> When Jesus saw their faith, he said to the paralytic, 'Son, your sins are forgiven.' (Mark 2.5)

> Happy are those whose transgression is forgiven. (Psalm 32.1)

In chapter 2 of his Gospel, Mark uses the powerful image of a sinner being lowered through a roof to show that anyone who seeks forgiveness will receive it. The symbol of a paralysed man (2.1–12) is employed to show how the questioning of Jesus cannot be forgiven because an unbelieving heart cannot stand in the face of God. This vignette supports the theme of metanoia (or repentance) by suggesting that to be forgiven, people must change in their hearts (beliefs) as well as their actions.

In the story of the paralysed man, Jesus seems to require more effort from the man seeking forgiveness than he did from the leper whose healing is described in Mark 1.40–45. The audience is so large that four men must lower the paralysed man down through the roof just to be near Jesus (2.3–4). Perhaps this is Mark's way of saying that a person can only be forgiven if that person truly wants to make an effort to change. Only after seeing the men's faith does Jesus heal the paralytic (2.5). Because Jesus claims to forgive the man's sins, the paralytic can represent any man without faith.

Both the death and resurrection of Christ and the negative portrayal of his disciples are important themes in the Gospel of Mark, but they are not directly applicable to the story of the paralysed man. I suppose it could be inferred that the disciples were not fulfilling their duties well enough, that they were being lazy; a helpless paralysed man could hardly make his way to Jesus, yet they did nothing to help. The scribes, who do not accept Jesus as the Messiah, become outraged and accuse him of blasphemy, because only God can forgive sins (Mark 2.6–7).

Lent is a time for reflection on the inner shape of our spiritual lives; a time to consider our lives and what we might want to change. As we look at the suffering of Christ we might want to reflect on the place of forgiveness in our lives. As we look at the picture of the healing of the paralysed man in Mark 2 we might want to consider our sins and the grace that comes from forgiveness.

Much of the work of a priest is hidden. It consists of private and personal conversations within which, through listening, one attempts to offer pastoral care. People come and go; conversations take place about all aspects of human life and its attempts to embrace hope and peace. Sometimes there are real moments of grace, moments when growth emerges; most of the time, though, it is almost impossible to know what difference these hours of sharing make. Priests are not alone in this task. Mothers, hospital cleaners, shop assistants and volunteers in charity shops are among those who listen. We too listen to others, to ourselves and to God. What difference does this activity make?

In life one needs to be careful about looking for results. Much is hidden, unknown and beyond our control. I share this reflection because one of the most difficult dimensions of the human experience that I have encountered in pastoral care is forgiveness.

I wonder, do you find it difficult to forgive, to let go of hurts and pains? If someone does us harm, how do we forgive? Let go? Forgive and forget? The reality of this goes deeper; faced with our own failures and mistakes, can we forgive ourselves? What we do with our own guilt – and sometimes with human guilt – can become so acute that it paralyses us.

Body, mind and spirit are interrelated: dysfunction, unforgiving hearts and a guilt-ridden sense of self can affect us physically. Psalm 32 was written by a man who was rejoicing with happiness because he had been liberated from a pressure so acute that it was making him ill.

What was this pressure? Guilt? Unresolved feelings of resentment about someone who had done him harm? If we look at the first few verses of Psalm 32 the writer tells of the debilitating illness from which he suffered. His bones were aching and his strength was sapped. Having given the diagnosis, the author switches to a personal testimony of repentance. He confesses his sin fully to God. The speed of God's grace is stunning. No wonder the psalmist begins rejoicing and singing!

The forgiven sinner's joy took several forms. It resulted in the writing of this psalm, which opens with resounding declarations of spiritual truth. We can be happy because God forgives us our sin; we receive forgiveness from him.

The message of the psalm is that God the Father embraces his penitent children with loving intimacy. In return those children adore their Father because he has freed them from their guilt and given them a new start in life. We share in the author's personal story of a God-centred journey to forgiveness.

Action, conversation, questions, prayer

Action

Can you find some wilderness time to be in the presence of God each day during Lent?

Conversation and questions

- Are there people you refuse to forgive?
- Which 'wild beast' prowls around your life? How do you deal with the 'beasts' in your life?
- Take some time to consider what parts of your life need the healing of God's forgiveness.

Prayer

We thank you for the generosity of your embrace.
Give us help to forgive,
as you forgive us in Jesus Christ.
In the light of your Holy Spirit
show us the possibilities of a life
full of new beginnings.
Amen.

5

Passion – Holy Week

Exploring the text

The Revised Common Lectionary's decision to intersperse Mark's Gospel with John's Gospel is nowhere more frustrating than in Holy Week. As we noted in the Introduction, Mark's Gospel builds from the moment that John the Baptist bursts on to the stage in chapter 1 to Jesus' final cry on the cross. For obvious reasons, each of the Gospels focuses on the cross as the event in which Jesus' ministry finally comes into focus. This is especially true of Mark. The second half of Mark's Gospel lies under the shadow of the cross, and of what this will mean not only for Jesus but also for those who follow him. It is therefore frustrating that this vitally important part of Jesus' life and ministry is covered in the Lectionary not in the words of Mark but in those of the fourth Gospel, whose theology of the cross is very different from Mark's. Indeed the only place where Mark's account of Jesus' death is given as an option at all is in the reading of the Liturgy of the Passion which some churches use on Palm Sunday.

Jesus' triumphal entry into Jerusalem

Jesus' last week began in spectacular style with his triumphal entry into Jerusalem on a donkey. All the way through Mark's Gospel our attention has been attracted by the differing responses to Jesus. As we noticed in the Introduction, the authorities nearly always reacted negatively towards Jesus, the crowd with amazement and wonder and the disciples with approval but bemusement. In contrast, various individuals, out of the depth of their need, recognized in Jesus someone who could save them. It is hardly surprising, then, that one of the major focuses of Mark's version of Jesus' entry into Jerusalem is the response to him of those around him.

The story of the entry into Jerusalem functions on two levels. On the surface it is simply the culmination of the whole of Jesus' ministry. Jesus has at last reached the moment to which the whole of his ministry has been building and now, at least for a while, he receives the recognition of the crowd who greet him not with amazement but with acclamation. On a deeper level, however, the story is even more important than this. The words with which the crowd greet Jesus are profoundly significant. They are a paraphrase of Psalm 118.25–26, 'Save us, we beseech you, O LORD! O LORD, we beseech you, give us success! Blessed is the one who comes in the name of the LORD. We bless you from the house of the LORD', although this is a little hard to see in the English translation. The word *Hosanna*, which is so important in Christian worship, appears in Hebrew only in Psalm 118.25. It means, literally, 'save now' and so is translated into the English version of Psalm 118 as 'Save us'. When the Gospel writers wrote the account of Jesus' entry into Jerusalem they did not translate the Hebrew word into Greek but put it in Greek letters still in its Hebrew form, so English translators leave it in its original Hebrew form as 'Hosanna'.

Thus the crowd were singing from Psalm 118 as they surrounded Jesus on his procession into Jerusalem. This is both unremarkable and extremely important. It is unremarkable because Psalm 118 forms a part of a collection of psalms called the Hallel Psalms (Psalms 113—118), so called because they praise God (*Hallel* being the Hebrew word for praise) for all that he has done. These were traditionally sung – and are still sung by Orthodox Jews – on major festivals. At the time of Jesus, it is thought, the Hallel Psalms would have been sung by the pilgrims on the journey to Jerusalem to worship God; they were particularly sung on pilgrimages to Jerusalem for the great festival of the Passover. Therefore, on one level, the singing of Psalm 118 by the crowd as they entered Jerusalem for the Passover is entirely unremarkable. It would probably have happened every year. What is remarkable, however, is that they sang it to a particular person: to Jesus. As well as being a Hallel Psalm, this psalm was also connected to the Davidic kingship and, by the time of Jesus, to the active expectation that a David-like figure would come and save God's people.

The psalm itself sets the scene for an expectation like this. Psalm 118 seems to record a victory by an unknown Davidic king against his enemies. The first 18 verses set down the king's account of the battle he faced and how God saved him; the rest of the psalm recounts his arrival at the temple to give thanks to God for that salvation, beginning in verse 19, 'Open to me the gates of righteousness', with the king's request to the priests to open the gates of the temple to him so that he can come and praise God. This is met in verse 26 with a blessing given to him by the priests: 'Blessed is the one who comes in the name of the LORD. We bless you from the house of the LORD.' The significance of Mark's account is that Jesus, just like that Davidic king, went straight to the temple upon his arrival in Jerusalem but he received no acclamation from the priests – or any of the leaders of the people. Indeed, far from it, the leaders even sought to arrest him and have him killed. The way that Mark sews together the use of Psalm 118 throughout chapters 11 and 12 reminds readers of Jesus' true identity and of the leaders' inability throughout the whole Gospel to see him as he was.

Jesus' death

As we noted in Chapter 3, Mark's story of Jesus' life reaches its climax with Jesus' death and the centurion's acknowledgement of him as 'God's Son'. This is not the only important feature of Mark's crucifixion narrative, however. Each of the Gospels brings out a different element of Jesus' death. In Mark it is a moment of utter darkness. Jesus' friends have all deserted him – even the unnamed young man has run away naked (14.33–72); the crowd have finally made up their minds and, no longer amazed by Jesus, they are now calling for his death (15.8–15); darkness lies over the whole land (15.33) and Jesus' cry from the cross is one of utter despair: 'My God, my God, why have you forsaken me?' (15.34).

And yet, even in the midst of the despair, Mark points us to glimmers of hope. Jesus' cry from the cross, while clearly coming from the depths of despair, offers hope. It is a quotation from the opening of Psalm 22, a psalm that begins in the depths of despair as the psalmist grieves for the way that he is treated by those around him who mock him, 'make mouths' at him and shake their heads (v. 7; cf. Mark 15.20, 29), and is so badly off that even his mouth is dry (v. 15; cf. Mark 15.23) and his enemies divide his clothes between them (v. 18; cf. Mark 15.24). Despite all this, however, the psalmist is confident that God will come and save him (Psalm 22.21, 24) and that the whole earth shall remember God and turn to him (22.27), and he ends, 'To him, indeed, shall all who sleep in the earth bow down; before him shall bow all who go down to the dust, and I shall live for him. Posterity will serve him; future generations will be told about the Lord, and proclaim his deliverance to a people yet unborn, saying that he has done it' (22.29–31). It seems, then, that Psalm 22 lies behind the whole of the crucifixion narrative in Mark and that, woven into this story of despair, are the golden threads of hope.

These golden threads are highlighted even more by the fact that, although we think Jesus has been utterly abandoned by his friends, after he dies the centurion acknowledges that he was the Son of God (Mark 15.39). Moreover, we discover that some of the women who followed him have not left him after all (15.40). Indeed Mark's narrative of Jesus' crucifixion tells us something significant about discipleship as a whole.

Discipleship, as the way of the cross, can be expected to display the same traits as Jesus' crucifixion. Just as his vocation was to the way of the cross, so also God calls us to the same way. Just as his own death was an event of despair laced with hope, so too we should remember that even in the darkest moments, God sends signs of hope.

Imagining the text

These next pieces imagine characters from Mark's Passion narrative as they reflect on their experience of the death of Jesus and its significance in their lives since, as its meaning within God's purpose of salvation for the world becomes clearer to them.

In the first piece the centurion who oversaw the execution of Jesus at Golgotha (Mark 15.22–39) meditates on his exclamation as Jesus died on the cross: he is the first of many Gentiles to be converted to faith in God through the revelation of Jesus as Christ crucified.

The second piece imagines the thoughts of the women disciples who witnessed the suffering and death of Jesus, standing some way off from Golgotha itself (15.40–41). The poem evokes their sense of pain and failure as they were separated from him after so many days and years of faithfully keeping him company, and of how they can witness to the uniqueness of Jesus in a distinctive way from this sense of distance and disappointment.

Witnesses at the cross

The centurion explains his exclamation:
'Truly this man was God's Son'

It was not the simple fact of a death that had me speaking out. I am not given to exclamation or outburst: feelings are not part of the equation for me when I'm in role, as I was that day. You should realize that for a military man crucifixion is a daily occurrence, an administrative duty, a small-time operation – some days there were scores of them one after another when the courts had been busy. A soldier becomes accustomed to executions: the squalid display of agony, strung out systematically to terrorize the populace; it's a kind of theatre, and I'd seen the play of horror time after time. Furthermore, I had seen greater deaths than the kind which happened at Golgotha; I mean the battlefield, the heroic sacrifice of fine soldiers defending their homeland, extending the reach of the empire with their blood – and I have risked my own life too, time after time, in loyal service. So it was not a ceremonial deployment that had me facing criminals for hours on end as they screamed and muttered their way to oblivion: death was integral to my profession, a tool of my trade – and every nerve and fibre of my own body was ready to fight to the death if required, and at my command hundreds of men at a time would risk their all.

Perhaps it was this military discipline which had shaped me over the years that gave me a sense that something was different in this particular death: his distinction, dedication, a kind of project reaching its culmination that day outside the city. This was a man who seemed to carry the world with him; not some criminal wretch getting his just deserts. My God, how they would howl out their innocence, lying dogs – but not him, his energy was focused somewhere else. I'm not saying for one moment that he was protected from the pain, or that there was less of it for him, or that his was a different kind of death from the one we designed. Like all the others, for him there was the ripping of the flesh, the baking in the sun, the humiliations and exposure, the wracking limbs, the thirst . . . There was nothing heroic or calm or untouched about that pain – it was like hours of scalding, searing, tearing apart, a death just as the system intended, an officially sanctioned, torturous end. But with him there were exceptional happenings, what we came to think of as special signs – first the darkened sky, as if creation itself was deeply disturbed, and then later we learnt about the strange disruptions in the temple . . .

But what struck me at the time was what any duty officer's nose for crowd control would tell him: the particular hostility of the authorities, the rage he drew from the crowd, the followers clotted here and there at a distance; these things put me on edge. And then towards the end his calling out to Israel's God, his quoting the psalm with absolute intention, such presence of mind, such spirit, as if the agony and utter loneliness were held for him within a crucible of faith – agony, sure enough, but somehow offered in trust, held out, cried out, like a sacrifice. It was as if he were making a gift of himself. It was as if he pulled God down into that terrible place, the place of ordinary horror, everyday pain.

As I say, I am not given to outbursts when doing my duty, but that day there was a pull deep in my guts, an exceptional quality to this particular dying, and I made my exclamation. Facing him there on that torturing wood, staring into his agony, I became the first of many to find God drawing close through the pain of his cross.

The women who stood at a distance from the cross

We stood at some distance,
Relieved, to be honest, that the soldiers kept us away;
Wanting to be closer, we encountered a barrier within
Holding us back.

Having been so near to him day after day
In Galilee, companions on almost all his travels,

This was one journey we could not make with him:
Golgotha was for him alone, we came to understand that
in time,
But on that day simply to witness was like a death itself
for us.
Oh, how we longed to cherish him,
To comfort, soothe, to save him;
To save him felt like our special task.
Measuring the distance in our minds since
The gap between his cross and the little huddle of disciples
we became,
Now we understand the beauty of the interval –
How it gave us sight of him, a perspective we needed to
gain.
Hanging there on the horizon, he became someone new
to us,
Irretrievably out of our care,
A sign for others.

We witness now, having seen from a distance.

Reflecting on the text

In this reflection we explore what the Passion of Christ might mean for us; how we might incorporate the Good Friday experience into our life and faith.

Love without pain is a lie

It must be easier for religious people, says a therapist working with the dying and bereaved: 'The assurance of eternal life must help you cope with death.' I was reminded of a chaplaincy colleague who declined to come to our Good Friday service because it was too upsetting. Her honesty was shocking, but no less than that of Christians who celebrate the joy of Easter without any attention to the waiting, the pain, and the suffering of Christ's Passion and death. We forget Holy Saturday, the entombment and the time of absolute loss, which is filled with the activity of getting ready for Easter.

Theology expressed in the liturgy of the Church can shape all parts of our lives. We seek to offer glimpses into how God would have us be in Christ. As we prepare to journey from Maundy Thursday through to Easter Sunday, we should consider how to incorporate the Good Friday experience into our life and faith.

Specifically, these days can help people reflect in the light of faith about the nature of loss, change, dying and death. One of my earliest childhood memories centres on the death of my great-grandmother in a mining village in the north-east of England. I was about five years old. When she died, the family kept vigil, and the only job the undertaker had was to leave the coffin at the house. The family did the rest, and her body lay in the front room as neighbours and friends came and went. I remember a relative lifting me up to say goodbye and touching her cold face. I thought how amazingly peaceful she looked.

Modern death is very different, of course. As a result, we are impoverished. We push it away and distance ourselves from it. There seems little chance of much intimacy in our mourning. The cold space in the modern crematorium allows us to see, but not to touch – somehow distancing us from the realities of dying.

In fact, however, we are dying all the time, and we must ask ourselves how our Easter faith helps us with this reality. As soon as we are born, we begin to die. We all live and grow, but before us lies the reality of the end of our life. We can deny or avoid it, but our lives are an amazing mixture of living and dying: a continual process of movement, change, losses and gains.

The child in us has to die before we become an independent teenager. Parents have to learn to let go of their children, and take risks by giving them freedom and choice. These dyings and deaths can lead to new life – the pattern of growth into new life by ways of embracing our diminishments and death.

We might consider our lives in the light of those losses. I never get used to parting either from people or from places. The places where I have lived and worked twine themselves around my heart like ivy around a tree trunk. Every corner has a memory that can tug at the heart. Leaving places is difficult, but, unless we part from one stage, we cannot begin in another.

Growth can begin with letting go. We might consider those parts of our life experience that we hold on to. Our lives can be enriched with broader sympathies and a feeling of hope, if we give space to reflecting on the changes that have shaped our lives.

For Christians, the pattern of living and dying, of death and resurrection, is given meaning by the life, death and resurrection of Jesus Christ. The final meal of Jesus and the Passion make up the central story that enables us to make sense of our lives. We tell and retell the story, attending to the pain, dereliction and death, so that we can find new life in Christ. In what happened to him, we see hope and meaning and truth for ourselves in our living and dying.

However much we might wish to avoid or deny the reality of death, time spent reflecting on the sheer cost of Christ's death offers hope. Images of the crucifixion give us a glimpse of a grotesque death endured in agony. It is a reflection of a God who has come down to the lowest part of our need. This is a complete offering of love and life for us. It becomes for us the new sanctuary of God's promise.

The crucified God is a paradox. He is a God at one with us in total self-giving, a God who knows the absence of God from the inside, and is able to overcome the power of sin and death. In this earthed sense, the Christian faith is incarnational.

It is embedded in a life, not in abstract ideas – in a life marked by a love made known to us in those hands pinned by nails to rough wood and then outstretched to embrace the world. Only a God who so engages with us and can bring us salvation is the living hope for which our world longs. Good Friday offers us the opportunity to engage with the reality of death in us and around us. The promise on the cross is that, in and through loss, through befriending our death, there lies the possibility of a surrender to and intimacy with God. We need, therefore, to learn to become less strong, less confident, less well defended, less identified with our own idea of God.

There is a tyranny that comes from our desire to hold on to certainty at all costs, eliminating paradox and contradiction. 'Sermons are for answering questions, not asking them', a colleague challenged me. Faith can enable us to open up and dig deep; to explore and change. Our befriending of change and loss is part of our attentiveness to the meaning of the cross and to the promptings of the Spirit. This is a pilgrimage to a place of honesty, humility and vulnerability.

It is a popular lie that there can be love without pain, or love without sacrifice, or that the word 'passion' signifies only the pursuit of pleasure. Such passion is fantasy, and will, in the end, die. True love is love that suffers, and this we find in the love of God which is the Passion of Christ.

Christ gave himself to the waiting and the Passion and the death. In his sacrifice, our human world of created values and relationships is challenged, so we can learn that dying strengthens our living. The awareness of limitations and the provisionality of much of life, especially our own mortality, is an expression of living, of healthy-mindedness, as we become more integrated in ourselves.

Perhaps we might consider our own deaths, too, on Holy Saturday, taking time to reflect on what shape our dying might take. We might focus on putting our affairs in order, perhaps by making a will or leaving clear instructions for our funeral. Our embracing of the reality of these practical matters is a spiritual task. It gives our living a sensitivity, an immediacy, a seriousness and an innocence. This can open up new dimensions about what we hope for, and who we want to become.

Befriending death finds its goal in making the dying experience explicit. We are not victims of dying, and it does not victimize us. We can, however, be victims of shallow, distorted attitudes to dying. Dying and death are not separate events: they shape our humanity and our spirituality. Dying is about learning how to give up what we have embodied – sacrificing control, so that we can be less fearful.

Being alive is about embracing our humanity, our flesh, our boundedness. We need to learn to live and die in a way that helps us better understand ourselves and all we stand for. Our engagement in the prayers and silence of our worship – a closer examination of the nature of our death in our believing – can enable our pilgrimage to lead us into new places.

Action, conversation, questions, prayer

Action

Find out more about one charity that seeks to alleviate human distress and suffering. Promote what you discover in your church.

Conversation and questions

- Think of a major change or crisis that has occurred in your life. How did you negotiate that change?
- What aspects of life is our society afraid of?
- Imagine your funeral. What would be said in the address about the place of faith in your life?

Prayer

Lord Jesus Christ,
you humbled yourself in taking the form of a servant,
and in obedience died on the cross for our salvation:
give us the mind to follow you
and to proclaim you as Lord and King,
to the glory of God the Father.
Amen. *Common Worship*

6

Easter

Exploring the text

Probably one of the best-known features of Mark's Gospel is its ending – or, depending on your perspective, its lack of ending. Unlike the other Gospels, the accounts of resurrection in Mark are sparse in the extreme. In Matthew an angel appears to Mary Magdalene and 'the other' Mary, followed by an appearance of Jesus to the two women and a second one to the disciples in Galilee at what has become called the great commission (Matthew 28). In Luke, similarly, two angels appear to Mary Magdalene, Joanna and Mary the mother of James (plus some other unnamed women) to announce the resurrection; this incident is followed by the well-loved account of Jesus' appearance to the two on the road to Emmaus and to the gathered group of disciples in Jerusalem (Luke 24). John has even more: there is the appearance of Jesus to Mary Magdalene in the garden, then to the disciples all gathered together (without Thomas), then again with Thomas, and finally the appearance on the shore of Galilee (John 20—21).

They ran away

In contrast, Mark's account of the resurrection, probably the oldest and most reliable of the Gospel accounts, is brief in the extreme. Mary Magdalene, Mary the mother of James, and Salome go to the tomb to embalm Jesus' body. There they meet a young man (whom we presume to be an angel) who instructs them to go and tell the disciples that Jesus has risen from the dead. Instead they are filled with fear and run away. The ending is abrupt in the extreme: the final sentence reads literally in Greek 'they were afraid for'.

This seems to be an odd ending to a Gospel and has, over the years, been the subject of much discussion. So much so, in fact, that there are alternative endings to the original text: some amend verse 8, others add the ending on to the end of Mark as it stands. One is very short and clearly intended simply to tie up the loose ends left by verse 8; it explains that the women reported all these instructions briefly to Peter's companions and that, afterwards, 'Jesus himself sent out through them, from east to west, the sacred and imperishable proclamation of eternal salvation.'

The other is longer and is printed in many English translations as 16.9–20. With very few exceptions the majority of New Testament scholars do not believe either ending to be by Mark. Instead a growing number of scholars think that Mark's Gospel was intended to end at 16.8, whereas others argue that there was a more complete ending but it is now lost.

Since there is no evidence for an original longer ending, it seems to be most sensible to deal with the ending we have and to assume that Mark did, in fact, intend the Gospel to end as abruptly as it does in 16.8. Those who want to say that the Gospel must have gone on longer point to the ugly usage of the word 'for' in Greek: as we noted above, the Greek ends 'they were afraid for'. In reality, however, this is only ugly in English not in Greek. In Greek the word 'for' is one of those that must come second in a sentence – grammatical rules insist upon it. Grammatically, then, this is the only way for Mark to end a two-word sentence which includes 'for'. It is certainly dramatic but it also seems to fit quite well with the whole theme of Mark's Gospel.

Responding to Jesus

Throughout Mark's Gospel one of the abiding questions has been how people will respond to Jesus. This is set up early on in the Gospel by the use of the parable of the sower (Mark 4.1–20), which unusually is interpreted by Jesus. In the interpretation we see that the key theme is response. Some do not respond at all; some respond and then die away; others respond and give forth fruit. Mark adds to this picture throughout the Gospel, introducing us to groups who reject Jesus immediately (the authorities); those who are amazed but who seem not to be able to go beyond this (the crowd); and those who follow Jesus but do not understand him (the disciples). We add into this the numerous meetings between Jesus and individuals who respond to him out of their need. The fleeing of the women seems, once more, to fit into this pattern. They, like the disciples, go so far but no further. They, unlike the disciples, have not abandoned Jesus – Mark tells us (15.40) that they were present throughout the crucifixion – and they have now come to continue their service to him in death. But, overwhelmed by the enormity of what they have heard, they now flee.

There is a great forgiveness in this. It is as though Mark is reminding us that even the earliest followers – perhaps especially the earliest followers – failed in their discipleship (and if Christian tradition is correct in ascribing the source of Mark to Peter, then this rings even more true as a message). Even the earliest followers did not quite respond to Jesus as they might have hoped. You might think that this is a depressing message but in fact the opposite is the case. We who read Mark's Gospel today know that the women might have fled straight away, but that eventually they did tell someone what the angel had said to them – otherwise we wouldn't be reading about it now. It is very easy to assume that we must respond to Jesus perfectly on all occasions or risk being a failure. Mark's Gospel reminds us that this is not the case. The earliest followers of Jesus were as imperfect as we are – and still the good news of Jesus spread to the ends of the earth.

What Mark's Gospel reminds us is that God in God's great goodness invites us to join in with the 'good news of Jesus

Christ, the Son of God' but is not entirely dependent on our doing so. God considers us to play a very important role in the spreading of the good news of Jesus, but if we don't – if, like the women, we flee – God is still God and Jesus is still risen from the dead. The good news will spread with or without our involvement. Jesus calls us to follow him and expects from us great things, but if our response is less than perfect the good news remains and will spread anyway.

If 16.8 is in fact the intended ending for Mark's Gospel, it fits well with the rest of the Gospel and offers a challenge as well as reassurance. The moment has come when all can be revealed. The women are now told to 'go, tell'. For the first time all the pieces of the jigsaw about Jesus are available. They have seen his life and ministry, they have seen his death and now are told of his resurrection. We too know all we need to know about Jesus – so what will we do? How will we respond? The challenge resounds to each reader of the Gospel. Will we respond by following or by fleeing? However, if it should happen that our response is at first flight and not following, all is not lost. This is exactly how the earliest followers of Jesus responded, and still the good news of Jesus Christ, the Son of God, spread to the ends of the earth.

Imagining the text

'Divine synergy' is the last word

We have taken note of the abrupt way Mark ends his Gospel and there remains a challenge to us to ask how our discipleship might play its part in the sharing of good news. As we have seen, the final sentence of Mark's Gospel – at least in some versions – runs thus: 'And they went out and proclaimed the good news everywhere, while the Lord worked with them and confirmed the message by the signs that accompanied it' (16.20).

In this final section (added subsequently by a different author), the missionary experience of the early Church becomes a commentary on the transforming power of the gospel at work in the lives of those who first witnessed to Jesus, crucified and risen. For the very disciples who had betrayed, abandoned and disbelieved Jesus, who were dumb-struck with terror, these same failed disciples proclaimed him as Lord, and are a model for the Church. Disciples do not do this alone, but with the Lord who is 'working with them', in what could be called divine synergy.

In the following imaginary letter to Christians who have come to believe through the witness of inadequate disciples, the follower of Jesus who as a young man fled naked from the garden of Gethsemane when Jesus was arrested (Mark 14.51–52) describes his meeting with the women who also fled in terror from the empty tomb (16.8), and reflects on the power of Jesus at work in their flawed lives since then (16.20).

Easter

Dear friends in Christ,

Now that it is Easter once again, and we are celebrating together each day the resurrection of our Lord, allow me as the Elder who first brought to you the good news of Jesus, to look back to the first Easter I experienced, and to take stock of what the good Lord has done in and through my life. I never thought that I would have formed a church; indeed, there was a time when I did not have the confidence or self-respect to belong to any kind of community, let alone teach and pastor a flock. But I owe so much to the healing Spirit of Christ at work among us, sustaining and extending what we do in his name.

And I owe a great deal to those women who first brought to me the good news of his rising again. Not that it felt like good news immediately, and not that they used words at first. To begin with it was turmoil, confusion; but it was their fear and their silence and their absolute disarray that helped me understand they had encountered something authentic and disturbing, something of Jesus. I saw in those women the mysterious work of Christ. For when they came rushing in from their first visit to his tomb, breathless from the running and utterly speechless, trembling, I thought to myself, 'It's him! It's him!' I knew that for certain because, friends, I also had run away.

I said to them: 'Sisters, I know your fear. I too was terrified.'

That first Easter it was Magdalene, and Mary mother of James, and Salome – none of them women easily thrown off course; to see them so bewildered was a kind of relief to me, being ashamed as I was of what had taken place a few days earlier. I thought, 'We have become siblings, brother and sisters of the same Jesus-type disruption.' And it was true: he turned our lives upside down again and again, but in every storm he walked alongside us and pointed us forward beyond our guilt towards a new horizon.

There was guilt of course, that first Easter, as there is every Easter. You see I must confess that I fell short on every level, not only in the difficult times of his arrest and trial and execution, but even after it was all over. I had expected to be haunted by the memories of failure, to be crippled with guilt. Seeing the women in such a state, I assumed that they too must be running away from the awful things that had happened to him, escaping the painful truths within themselves, the shame and regret.

Like them, I had been with him in those last days in Jerusalem – not a member of his inner circle like them, you understand, but a person on the margins, fascinated by his teaching and inspired by all he did, yet still on the edge. I had plans to get more involved, to put myself forward and ask if

I might speak with him, find out more of what he was about, maybe even make some kind of commitment. I was young, there was so much to know and to understand, so many different paths from which to choose; I thought I had sufficient time to make a considered decision. I was cautious, but even so I was drawn to him and could not put his teachings out of my mind. So I would follow most days, moving about from place to place with the crowd who gathered round him, listening and being amazed, but always in the shadows.

That's how I ended up being there the night he was arrested: I was following – well, sort of following – more lurking really, wanting to be close to him without being counted in. I was near enough to see what he did at the supper, how he took the bread and then the wine and said those strange words about his body and his blood and new wine in the kingdom of God. I heard him say to them, the ones closer in, how they would betray him. I heard him insist that even Peter, the one who was always so vehement, would disown the very man he said he would defend to the death. Actually, they all said the same – I heard them make their promises as they walked in the night to the Mount of Olives – and I was relieved not to have to give that kind of undertaking. In Gethsemane I was close enough to see him praying, though I was just a little distant from the rest as they huddled together in the chill night. I fell asleep too; we all did. I have tried to tell myself that I didn't count, not my little snooze. But I saw his hurt.

I saw many things: the officials come through the dark with their soldiers and police. I saw Judas give that cruel kiss of his and call him 'Teacher'. I saw all that vile charade of love, and then the squabble with the High Priest's servant. I wasn't one of those standing close, but I was close enough to hear the calm in his voice and the way he challenged the temple authorities about why they were treating him like a criminal when everything he had ever done was open and truthful. I heard him speak, saying about the Scriptures being fulfilled – and now I'm not sure whether it was *that* which made me run, I mean his tone of resignation and the way he seemed to give his whole self over to them – was it that which terrified me, or the stampede of the others scattering like sheep?

When I bolted the soldiers grabbed me, and as they held me in place I could hardly believe the surge of panic which powered my escape – the sheer cold energy of desperation deep in my guts. I leapt to get away from them, from him, from any association with that Jesus.

You know the story told now in all our churches, of my linen robe unravelling, how they could not keep a grip on me, and then my long run naked into the night, my long run away from the authorities, from his followers . . . my naked run from Jesus. I left the linen in the garden of course; I dare not go back in the morning myself, and unlike the women, I hid all day in my house. But I sent my servant to Gethsemane to see if it were there among the olive trees and bushes. He said some wretch had picked it up and laundered it – selling it for new on the roadside, with its expertly sewn seams, unmistakable quality. When the worst was done on Golgotha, on the Sabbath eve, imagine my horror when Joseph the learned Arimathean told me how he had courageously persuaded Pilate to release the broken body, and bought some linen for the burial off a roadside stall, in a desperate hurry, pure linen he said, unused he said, with exquisitely stitched seams. I said nothing to Joseph, of course, but it was torture to think that the body of Jesus was wrapped in my discarded garment, the one in which I abandoned him. He went into the grave wearing my disloyalty tight round him, my fear, my shroud.

The thought of having to live with that kind of guilt might have finished me: the death of Jesus in which I could not share, nor understand. But I saw the same dumb, terror-driven fright in those women when they fled the tomb; it was then I knew that there was another encounter with Jesus, with his power to heal and to make new.

This is why, dear friends, in all our telling of the Gospel stories, we have never tried to hide from you our failures as his disciples. Those memories of failure are part of the story of his resurrection. It is not perfect people Jesus calls to follow him; it is the ones like me, flawed disciples – the ones who have wanted to run away, who have found it difficult to speak, who have been bewildered by their encounter with him – we're the ones with whom he chooses to work.

May the peace and healing of the risen Lord be yours this Easter. Amen.

From your loving Pastor . . . the man who ran away.

Reflecting on the text

Sharing the good news of Christ is challenging. We might remember the tragic words of G. K. Chesterton: 'Christianity has not been tried and found wanting; it has been found difficult and not tried.' It is easy for us like the early disciples to run away, to draw the narrative to a quick close and leave the work for others. The questions that we have asked from the text remain: We too know all we need to know about Jesus – so what will we do? How will we respond? The challenge resounds to each reader of the Gospel. Will we respond by following or by fleeing?

In the next two reflections these questions are earthed in two dimensions of the good news. First we consider the nature of Easter joy and ask about the nature of our identity in Christ. In this reflection I share the surprise of joy I experienced within a moment of spiritual awareness at an Easter vigil. This forms part of a conviction that Easter Christians always entertain the possibility of joy when being open to the new.

Easter joy

It is Easter morning 1984. I have journeyed through part of Lent and Holy Week and listened and prayed a familiar story. We gathered in a convent chapel set in acres of Kent countryside in the darkness to affirm, proclaim and celebrate the resurrection of Christ. In a few brief seconds something remarkable happened for me. As the priest lifted the communion vessels I became aware that the darkness had given way to morning. The sun rose and light filled the chapel. By the time we said the Lord's Prayer we were joined by the birds in a chorus of sound. The ordinary cycle of night and day took on a new meaning – we experienced what we were proclaiming. Darkness had given way to light; Christ conquered death. The new life of Christ was made present in the broken bread and outpoured wine. It was an experience of profound joy, quiet but clear, light but holy. The celebration of life offered in this Easter Eucharist was transformative – a brief moment of pure joy that has carried me through many times of perplexity. Even that distant memory has the capacity for surprise and refreshing joy. That moment was a movement to being aware, of experiencing truth. I began to absorb in head and heart the powerful love that God offers us in Christ. It was a moment of harmony where the cry of thankfulness gave way to gratitude and joy.

The Christian story is a story built upon joy. We are and we should be a people who overflow with joy. This joy is a by-product of the deep gratitude that we all experience when we realize how much God loves us and when we accept God's invitation to become integral characters in God's story. Joy is a consequence of our sense of the beauty and wonder of God's presence with us.

The philosopher Friedrich Nietzsche, himself the son of a minister, expressed his concern about how we live out the Easter message: 'His disciples should look more redeemed.' A visit to our churches this weekend may give foundation for this criticism. Many Christians are surrounded by an air of heaviness, of oppressive sternness, of lack of humour and irony about themselves! If we were to find time for the transforming possibilities of worship, give more time to be aware of the power of love and joy, that power might find expression in our lives and churches.

This is not escapism. We know that in this life very little is certain and fixed. It is hard to keep the faith in a materialistic, distracted and busy world. Easter joy asks us to redraw our lives into a new way of seeing. This envisioning might happen when we consider how we understand God and where we look for the presence of God. More time spent with Scripture as a preparation for our Sunday worship, in silence, in giving expression to the parts of our lives that give us cause for delight – all these can help us experience the presence of God. I often place in my prayer book a list of the things that lift my heart towards joy. God can speak to us in and through these small actions. Joy can be nurtured through an embracing of doubt, honesty and openness. For all of us there are aspects of our faith that feel fragile and thin. As we are receptive to our questions about discipleship, so we foster an openness that can be a springboard into a deeper wisdom. Those early disciples found that the dawning of joy, freedom and release spilled out of their bewilderment, anguish and searching. We might want to share our spiritual journey in conversation with others, building up the trust to discover and be surprised by listening to each other.

We know that all of life is God's, and God is the creative ground of life. God meets us in the tapestry of our living and can work creatively through that meeting. The joy in God and the joy of life can belong together. Joy is born out of union with reality itself, especially when we open ourselves up to the new and unfamiliar. This may include getting to know Christians in different circumstances from our own, at home or abroad. It might mean opening up ourselves to something new in worship, whether in music or ways of praying.

We Christians do not easily change our minds about things, embrace new ideas, adopt new attitudes. It was Newman who said, 'Growth is the only evidence of life', and, 'To be perfect will be to have changed often.' How odd, then, that people pride themselves on the fixity of their beliefs. Joy might be about being open-minded and ready for surprises. When new ideas, new approaches to things, new discoveries about human nature come to us, they often come from the outside, and our experience challenges us to change. That Easter Eucharist taught me that nurturing faith is as much a matter of the heart as of the intellect. We often glimpse the truth of God through our readiness to open our heart to the divine movement of love. Some have found religious art as a way into a deeper comprehension of how the story of Christ can shape us. St George's, Windsor, maintains an Anglican choral tradition of sung services. Music can also bring things alive and help us to see things afresh.

Spending time looking and waiting and being opens the doors of perception. The hardest wood takes longest to grow. We should place ourselves in difficult situations and conversations where the risk of challenge and change is possible. This might mean looking at our 'Good Friday' wounds as part of learning to live with whatever has hurt us in the past. In contemplating these wounds, of love lost, of mistaken choices, of hurts caused, we learn to mend and have courage to move on. The obvious place to open oneself up to this joyful resurrection life is through our affinity with creation. But that change can emerge from the honesty of our struggle with living, people and modernity. There might be nobility in a tower block or estate of identical homes, dignity in the plea of the Big Issue seller, community among the commuters distracted by their mobile phones and computers. In this crucible of life God will bless us as we wrestle with a new or disturbing idea. This can produce passionate commitment, surprise and joy. Love that endures best took the longest to develop.

The element of joy in religion is prominent in the New Testament. It provides the foundation for happiness and pleasure. It is present in all levels of our striving for fulfilment. It requires a movement of heart and will; a choice to nurture this gift in self and others. It can emerge out of our struggle. We must be prepared to be surprised by the possibilities of our Emmaus journey. The stranger might lead us in unexpected ways of knowing. Our vulnerable hearts are the places where joy springs and informs the intellect. The joy of life is possible in pleasure and pain, in happiness and unhappiness, in ecstasy and sorrow. Above all it can surprise us when we open ourselves up for change.

Easter and the self?

On a journey back to my childhood home I was struck by a strong sense of discontinuity as well as continuity: of almost absolute familiarity and strangeness. We sometimes wonder what we are and what we've become. The question comes into sharper focus when we consider people who have committed terrifying crimes. The debates surrounding this question – of who we are and whether we can fundamentally change ourselves – continue to intrigue us. What does it mean to be uniquely and inalienably who we are? There is a consistency, an integrity of self and self-identity. Do we recognize the person God has made us, despite the many and sometimes baffling movements and changes of geography, work and even relationship that person has undergone?

Easter brings home to us the truth of the remark: we are uniquely and inalienably the person we are. Of course we change in character and appearance through time, but it is I, myself, to whom the change occurs. I look back to my childhood, go back to the house which was my home during my childhood and young adulthood; I know that I may not be the same person that I was in terms of knowledge or experience or appearances, but in a curious way I am the person who was that child. Our identity is persistent and has a life and continuity that defies those addicted to the postmodern chaos.

This is not to underestimate the difficulties and perplexities of being an Easter Christian. We may be vexed by doubt or sustained by faith: our lives may be affected by conflict or persecution: we may hide ourselves in anxiety and fear. But it is to us that these changes occur. Our world is unpredictable and fleeting but Easter and its power is offered to our self, to our soul, for salvation. The soul cannot be destroyed or spoiled or withered away. It is guaranteed by a God who does not change but abides for ever. God is impassable. God is timeless and unchanging.

We are invited to think something of this truth (albeit dimly, and with very inadequate language if we try to articulate it) in and through moments and occasions of absolute value. In these moments we affirm the absolute reality of God. When we bring the absolute (which we recognize in moments and occasions of truth and beauty and goodness) within the changing and time-bound, we begin to glimpse God through these partial experiences.

As we consider this in the context of Mark's Gospel and his narrative, it may seem rather remote and academic, even contradictory, as we encounter God in Christ. Mark gives us a picture of a glorious, unlimited and unchanging love. It is that stability that makes our own change and conversion possible, because there is a point of reference for it which is neither relative nor temporary.

The message of Easter is the movement of our lives, the steady transformation of our character into that love which we discern already to be the unchanging condition of God. Do we then ask to live with ourselves as we are, in our present character, through all eternity – or are we prepared to allow the risen life of Christ to work within us now, changing our character in the direction of love? This is the paradox of Easter – we begin to lose preoccupation with our self: it is to lose the self in order to find it again, secure in the practice of trust which is indeed a joy too great for words.

Action, conversation, questions, prayer

Action

Read Mark's resurrection account again and spend some time imagining some of the emotions experienced by the women as they ran away.

Conversation and questions

- What kind of emotions do you think were uppermost in the minds of the earliest disciples after Jesus' resurrection?
- Have you ever responded to God's call to you in a way that you later regretted?
- If you were asked to sum up 'Easter joy' what would you say?

Suggestions for prayer

- Pray for forgiveness for those times when you have not responded to God as you or God might have wanted.
- Give thanks for all that God has done in the world in Christ.

Prayer

God of glory,
by the raising of your Son
you have broken the chains of death and hell:

fill your Church with faith and hope;
for a new day has dawned
and the way to life stands open
in our Saviour Jesus Christ.
Amen. *Common Worship: Daily Prayer*

7

Ordinary Time

Exploring the text

The aim of Mark's Gospel is to introduce us to Jesus Christ, the Son of God. There are many ways in which we can encounter him – for example, through his calling of his followers or in the moments of great revelation at the baptism, transfiguration and crucifixion – but probably the best way to encounter Jesus in all his fullness is through his 'everyday life'. Jesus' everyday existence, however, is very different from our own: it is marked both by his teaching and by his miracles. It is very easy today to attempt to split Jesus' miracles and teaching apart. Miracles are something many people today feel uncomfortable about, so we focus much more attention on Jesus' teachings. Mark's Gospel, however, makes this rather difficult. Unlike Matthew and Luke, Mark does not give us large blocks of Jesus' teaching (such as the Sermon on the Mount in Matthew 5—7) but instead weaves it throughout the whole of the Gospel.

Jesus' teaching and miracles

Indeed one of the noticeable features of Mark is that in the Gospel Jesus' miracles are explicitly linked with his teaching. So, for example, in Mark 1.21–27, we find the story of Jesus' first casting out of a demon in the synagogue in Capernaum. At the start of the story the crowd are amazed by Jesus' teaching, but after the account of the casting out of the demon they attribute to him authority as well: 'They were all amazed, and they kept on asking one another, "What is this? A new teaching – with authority! He commands even the unclean spirits, and they obey him"' (1.27). In other words, Jesus' miracles are a part of his teaching because, just like the words that he uses, they tell us something about the kingdom of God.

In fact, the miracles of Jesus draw our attention to the fact that our understanding of teaching is far too small. We readily associate teaching with words, but it becomes clear in Mark's Gospel that Jesus teaches about the kingdom with the whole of his life. He shows us in the miracles that the God whose kingdom he proclaims is far more powerful than the things of this world that we fear the most. He shows us in his eating with outcasts that in God's kingdom the poor and marginalized are the greatest of all. He shows us in his interaction with people that God cares for all people no matter who they are, and most of all he shows us in his death the extent of that love.

Mark reminds us powerfully, then, that if we truly want to understand who Jesus was, we need to look at the whole of his life and not just at his words. His words are of course helpful and important, but they paint only half of the picture of Jesus.

Healings and miracles

Often when scholars explore Jesus' miracles they split them into two distinct types: healings and nature miracles. By this means they distinguish Jesus' healing of human beings from his control of nature. In one way, of course, this distinction is artificial and assumes that human beings are not a part of nature; in another way, however, it helpfully reminds us that there is something more to the healings than to the other nature miracles. By and large the nature miracles, like the stilling of the storm or the walking on water, tell us of Jesus' power over the natural world. These miracles are often reminiscent of creation. In Genesis 1 God imposed order on the chaos of the waters of the deep and so brought into being life as we know it. The nature miracles indicate that Jesus too has power over those forces of nature that are too great for human beings to control and can bring peace, harmony and the space for life in the world in which we live.

The healings have an additional dimension. In one way they are very similar to the nature miracles, in that they demonstrate that the Creator of the world still has the power to re-create and to bring life, but they communicate something much greater than this too. In our modern world it is easy to forget the stigma of illness that existed at the time of Jesus. The impact of illness in the first century was far greater than simply the illness itself. Illness – physical or mental – often meant exclusion from ordinary society. Temple laws dictated that those who were ill were no longer allowed to enter the temple and to sacrifice. People would have been cut off from the normal everyday life that others followed. The healings, then, didn't just entail the removal of physical, mental, emotional or spiritual impediments but a full reinclusion into society for those who would otherwise have been on its margins.

Thus Jesus' healings are about making people whole in every way possible: to meet them where they are and to draw them into the centre of a kingdom in which the last is first and the least greatest. Jesus' miracles re-create people, making them whole once more and restoring them to a proper relationship both with God and with their neighbours.

Healings and faith

Thus Jesus' healings reveal as much to us about who Jesus is as his other words and actions. As a result they are not simple 'wonder workings'. At the time of Jesus there were a number of people who the historian Josephus recounts as being renowned for the miracles that they did. Jesus' miracles were not like theirs. Their miracles were impressive, and were intended to impress. Jesus' miracles expressed something deep about who he was and were dependent on a recognition of this fact. He could only heal in the context of faith. He did no miracles where there was no expression of faith in who he was and who he had come to be in the world. Thus in his home town he was unable to do any 'deed of power' because they did not recognize him (Mark 6.1–6). He refused to give the Pharisees a sign because they asked out of curiosity not faith (8.11–13), and he only healed the daughter of the Syrophoenician woman once he had established the faith from which she spoke (7.24–30). The phrase 'your faith has made you well', literally 'your faith has saved you', is an expression of this. Jesus healed not to impress people but as an expression of who he was. Healing, then, involved mutual recognition: they of who he was and he of their faith. It was based in and arose out of relationship, and it is this which tells us so much about the real Jesus.

Imagining the text

This monologue allows one of the many characters healed by Jesus – Bartimaeus, the blind beggar of Jericho, who has his sight restored (10.46–52, Proper 25) – to reflect on his encounter with Jesus, and on the transformation he experiences through Jesus' ministry to him as a whole person, rather than as a broken individual who needs to be 'fixed'.

At this turning point in Mark's narrative, when Jesus journeys towards his Passion and death at Jerusalem, Bartimaeus models true discipleship: he chooses to use his new-found independence and freedom to follow Jesus in the way of discipleship on the road to the cross. In seeing with the eyes of faith, Bartimaeus will follow Jesus in walking the way of suffering and sacrificial obedience, a path which the other disciples have yet to discern or to choose for themselves, as they squabble over status and fail to understand the true nature of Jesus' leadership (10.32–45).

Bartimaeus sends a message home to his wife

I know you'll be furious with me; I should be at home celebrating with you and Timaeus and the rest of the family, not on my way to Jerusalem – but please give me a chance to explain. Not that I know exactly what to say, it's not easy to get my thoughts in order, let alone put them into words. I'm overwhelmed by colours, the shapes, the movement of things – clouds across the sky, wind in the trees, the faces of people, their eyes . . . All these wonderful things are dawning on me for the first time in many years. I'm seeing again. Yes, it's true! By now the news will have reached you that I have regained my sight. The teacher we had heard about, Jesus of Nazareth, he restored my sight! He came to Jericho as we were told he might, and what we had heard about him turned out to be true: Jesus the miracle-worker – he healed me!

I was sitting in my regular spot by the side of the Jericho–Jerusalem road, begging as usual with my cloak spread out in front of me, calling out for alms, and not doing too badly with more than the average amount of traffic passing by, a steady rain of coins falling on the cloth quite nicely. A big crowd came down the road out of the city – I'd not heard anything like it for a long time. People were really excited, talking and shouting, muttering and arguing with one another; it was like some kind of unofficial festival. There was a lot of religious talk. I asked what was going on, and they said that a holy teacher was passing through on his way to Jerusalem. When I asked, 'Who is it?' they said Jesus of Nazareth. Of course as soon as

I heard the name I started calling out, loud and persistent – that un-ignorable screeching I reserve for rich travellers and wedding parties. 'Jesus! Jesus!' I bawled, determined to get his attention.

The people with him told me to quieten down (typical religious types they were, with strict, icy voices, all regulations and no compassion . . .) but I wasn't going to take any notice of them. After all, what could they do? So I shouted louder, 'Jesus! Jesus!' and I got fired up with all the secret stories we had heard about him defeating the demons that have terrorized people for years, restoring chronic cases to full strength, bringing new life to all kinds of hopeless situations – I was desperate to get myself a moment with him, because of all the wonderful things we'd heard about him. I thought to myself, 'Come on, Bartimaeus, you can't miss an opportunity like this: Jesus the healer-man on your own patch, right in front of your face!'

So I did exactly what I was taught to do by the best beggars in Jericho when there was a rich man walking by, surrounded by his entourage and all the noise that accompanies important people: to break through all that company which keeps out people like us, the people on the pavement and in doorways, I called him something which was bound to soften his heart and flatter him. I tried to think of a fancy title which would oblige him to make some great show of generosity in order to be seen to live up to his reputation. As I thought of those stories of his teaching and his healing, his authority, I began to feel desperate – I wanted his compassion for myself, his attention, his concern, I wanted his mercy, like from a king or a prophet . . . (maybe even the mercy a wayward husband begs from his offended wife!). Then it slipped out, my title for him: 'Son of David'. Not one I'd heard him called before, not one I'd heard attached to any man I'd ever met or heard about: 'Son of

David' . . . that's what I heard myself calling him, an outrageous title for him, a mere carpenter from Nazareth . . . but it fitted him in my head as I called it out again, 'Jesus, Son of David!' really loud.

His cronies were absolutely furious with me and told me to pipe down, and the locals didn't want to hear my familiar voice – they tried to hush me in the hope they could catch some of what he was saying to his companions, but I wasn't going to miss my chance, and I called out even louder, 'Jesus, Son of David! Have mercy on me!' Everything went quiet, and they stopped walking, stopped talking – I guess *he* stopped, so of course they all did – and I heard him asking for me, telling them to fetch me, and they pushed me forward. All of a sudden I was something of a local hero, being patted on the back, encouraged by people who wanted to see what would come of it all. I got up in a hurry – please, my dear, don't shout at me, but I spilled all the money collected in my cloak as I flung it aside in my eagerness to get to him – I sprang towards him, right up to him – they helped me find my way – and he asked me directly what I wanted, what he could do for me. It sounds stupid to say so, arrogant even, given that I'm nobody important, but when he asked me what he could do for me, I felt like he really wanted to know, I felt that my concerns were absolutely at the heart of who he is. This Jesus seemed to lure out of me my deepest desire, as if the fulfilment of my fiercest longing lay in him, that he would teach me all the truth I need to know about God if I would only trust to him the things about myself I most long to be healed. 'My teacher,' I said to him, 'let me see again.' I put my whole being in his hands when I said those words to him; I gave myself to him, because I sensed that God was at work in whatever he would do with me. And I regained my sight that moment. He set me free: 'Go; your faith has made you well,' he said, as if he could see into my heart and all the trust that I had put in him, in God . . .

I'm saying all this, my dear, not to make excuses, but to explain. I know I should be back with you to live a different kind of life: no more begging, no more relying on the goodwill of others for what we need to get by. Soon I will be back there; but not yet. You have been the strong one for our family for so many years, and I have to ask you to carry on steering us for a little while longer yet. This new adventure is part of what it means for me to be well, to be whole and fully alive. I don't want to simply receive from Jesus; I want to participate in his life. Does it sound so strange that once I had my sight again, and saw him walking down that road towards Jerusalem, I had to follow him? Is it so strange to want to learn more, to share in his life? He set me free, and I found within my freed heart that my first choice was to be with him, and to go where he goes, and for his people to become my people. As soon as I could see, I wanted to be led by him, to walk in his way. What awaits us in Jerusalem I am not certain. After all, my choice is not to be certain, but to follow.

Reflecting on the text

A leper came to him begging him, and kneeling he said to him, 'If you choose, you can make me clean.' Moved with pity, Jesus stretched out his hand and touched him, and said to him, 'I do choose. Be made clean!' Immediately the leprosy left him, and he was made clean. After sternly warning him he sent him away at once, saying to him, 'See that you say nothing to anyone; but go, show yourself to the priest, and offer for your cleansing what Moses commanded, as a testimony to them.' But he went out and began to proclaim it freely, and to spread the word, so that Jesus could no longer go into a town openly,

> but stayed out in the country; and people came to him from every quarter. (Mark 1.40–45)

I wonder what it must feel like to be a leper. The only place I have encountered lepers in significant numbers is in India. Part of the distressing response to those begging for help is to shut them out, so as to distance their connection with us. 'I can't help one and not the others – it's impossible to deal with the system that produces so many beggars', is one of the ways in which we distance and protect ourselves. Perhaps a more common experience for us in this country is the predicament of the increasing number of homeless people. How often have we passed a young woman or man in a shop doorway asking for some change? How often have we made a decision to give? Or have we, as I myself have too often done, chosen to walk briskly on?

As a society we keep people trapped in and by our systems. We construct systems to keep the good in, keep them protected, and to keep the bad out. In the Gospel reading the leper is an outsider for good reason. He is a real threat to the good order of God's creation, an affront to a decent, clean, safe way of life. The leper has no choice or no freedom. Perhaps this is also true of those who find themselves homeless?

The Gospel challenges us to look at our lives in the light of the pity shown by Jesus. This is ultimately bad news. For to remain untouched by Jesus is to remain unclean, and to remain unclean is to be a certified outsider for ever, both in relation to society and to God. It is easy to be fooled by present-day perceptions. But are there attitudes within us that remain unclean, limits to our pity and compassion? Are we trapped by a system that keeps control by drawing the boundaries, leaving some on the inside and some on the outside?

The leper is freed by the outsider by choice. Strange as it may seem, the hope of the outsider does not rest on figuring out how to get 'in' with the system. That is an impossibility.

Rather, the outsider's hope is secured only as Jesus chooses to go out to him. And of course, by going out to the outsider, Jesus too becomes an outsider. Once Jesus chooses to help the outsider, the leper, then Jesus becomes an outsider by choice. And that is now where Jesus chooses to be found, on the outside, so that those who are cast out may be in the proximity of his compassionate touch.

This is about salvation – our salvation – and how we live within the good news of Jesus. Perhaps the good news of Jesus becomes good news for us only as Jesus' choice for us results in becoming also our choice for him. There is an old adage that says 'beggars can't be choosers'. While that is true with regard to life in the system, life within discipleship is different.

Jesus came precisely so that beggars like the leper, beggars like us, can be choosers: choosers of Christ, because Christ first chose us. In traditional biblical and Christian language, that choice is called faith; and it is nothing short of a life-changing confidence with regard to God.

God creates us with the endless capacity to choose and we are offered freedom to exercise that choice in our response to Christ. We should be thoroughly people of choice: free to live as Christ lives – for others. That fact is demonstrated by the paradoxical ending of the text. We, who are cleansed by Christ, are free either to keep or not to keep the commandments, depending on what is helpful.

Therefore we Christians are not automatons, even though our life is based on one who, through his death and resurrection, utterly opposed and discredited the law as a basis for holiness. Christians are perfectly free to choose to keep and support the work of the system when it is helpful to others. On the other hand, Christians are also free not to keep the commandments when it is not helpful, especially when the issue is the cleansing of outsiders.

When that is at issue, we (the cleansed) are perfectly free to touch and embrace the outsider, regardless of what the law may say. That's what the leper chose to do in our text. Having been cleansed, he chose to proclaim Christ freely. But as he did so – and as we do the same – we need to realize that we are acting outside the system, and that those who are trapped in the system will more than likely confirm their bondage by treating us as outsiders, as Jesus himself was treated. For us outsiders, cleansed by Christ, that is precisely our freedom, our cross – by choice.

Action, conversation, questions, prayer

Action

Try to encounter in a new way someone who is an 'outsider' to you – for example, ask the name of the person who sells you the *Big Issue*, or of a neighbour or church member who is familiar but not yet known. Meet that person in a new way.

Conversation and questions

- Who are the 'outsider' equivalents of the blind, the lepers and the lame in our society? How might we be being called to respond to them?
- What has being touched by Jesus meant in your life?

Suggestions for prayer

- Spend some time praying for those who find themselves outcasts at home, at work, in the country in which they live, etc.
- Make a conscious decision to 're-choose' Christ as he chose you, and offer this decision in prayer.

Prayer

Lord, you have taught us
that all our doings without love are nothing worth:
send your Holy Spirit
and pour into our hearts that most excellent gift of love,

the true bond of peace and of all virtues,
without which whoever lives is counted dead before you.
Grant this for your only Son Jesus Christ's sake,
who is alive and reigns with you,
in the unity of the Holy Spirit,
one God, now and for ever.
Amen. *Common Worship*

Copyright acknowledgements

The publisher and author acknowledge with thanks permission to reproduce extracts from the following. Every effort has been made to seek permission to use copyright material reproduced in this book. The publisher apologizes for those cases where permission might not have been sought and, if notified, will formally seek permission at the earliest opportunity.

'Blessed Lord, who hast caused all holy Scriptures', Collect, Second Sunday in Advent, The Book of Common Prayer. Extracts from The Book of Common Prayer, the rights in which are vested in the Crown, are reproduced by permission of the Crown's Patentee, Cambridge University Press.

'O Lord our God, make us watchful and keep us faithful', Post Communion, First Sunday of Advent, *Common Worship* (London: Church House Publishing, 2000). Extracts from *Common Worship* are copyright © The Archbishops' Council, 2000, and are reproduced by permission: <copyright@c-of-e.org.uk>

'Lord Jesus Christ, you humbled yourself', Post Communion, Palm Sunday, *Common Worship*.

'God of glory, by the raising of your Son', Collect, Morning Prayer on Sunday, *Common Worship: Daily Prayer* (London: Church House Publishing, 2005). Extracts from *Common Worship: Daily Prayer* are copyright © The Archbishops' Council, 2005, and are reproduced by permission: <copyright@c-of-e.org.uk>

'Lord, you have taught us', Collect, Second Sunday after Trinity, *Common Worship*.

Further reading and resources

There are many good commentaries on Mark's Gospel. The one you choose will be down to your own personal taste. The list below is not exhaustive but includes some of the best commentaries on Mark.

Lighter commentaries

Tom Wright, *Mark for Everyone*, 2nd edn (London: SPCK, 2001), in Wright's excellent series, The Bible for Everyone, combines clear exegesis with an easy to read style. Larry W. Hurtado, *Mark: New International Biblical Commentary* (Peabody, MA: Hendrickson, 1989), is also good and explores the complexities of some issues a little more than Tom Wright. The style is nevertheless still easy to read.

Although quite old now, D. E. Nineham's small commentary *Saint Mark*, new edn (Harmondsworth: Penguin, 1992), is packed with gems, and as it is easy and cheap to buy is well worth having on your shelf next to one of the newer volumes.

Medium-sized commentaries

Both Morna D. Hooker, *The Gospel According to Saint Mark* (Peabody, MA: Hendrickson, 2009), and Ben Witherington, *The Gospel of Mark: Socio-rhetorical Commentary* (Grand Rapids, MI: Eerdmans, 2001), present different but thoughtful angles on Mark's Gospel. Hooker's commentary represents the best of careful but relevant historical critical study of the Bible; Witherington is more interested in the social-scientific background of the Gospel. Both each in their own way provide new insights into the Gospel but do not have preachers in mind as their major audience.

Also good is John R. Donahue and Daniel J. Harrington, *The Gospel of Mark* (Collegeville, MN: Liturgical Press, 2005), which unlike

Hooker and Witherington aims to be both scholarly and relevant for preachers.

Heavyweight commentaries

For those who prefer a commentary based on the Greek text, the two best are Robert Guelich, *Mark 1—8:26*, Word Biblical Commentary vol. 34a (Nashville, TN: Thomas Nelson, 1989), and C. R. Evans, *Mark 8:27—16:20*, Word Biblical Commentary vol 34b (Nashville, TN: Thomas Nelson, 2001), or R. T. France, *The Gospel of Mark: A Commentary on the Greek Text* (Grand Rapids, MI: Eerdmans).

Other interesting books on Mark's Gospel

An unmissable commentary of a very different kind is Ched Myers, *Binding the Strong Man: A Political Reading of Mark's Story of Jesus*, 20th edn (Maryknoll, NY: Orbis, 2008), which understands Mark's Gospel as a political document and draws out insights from its narrative about the politics of Jesus.

Also good is Elizabeth Struthers Malbon, *Mark's Jesus: Characterization as Narrative Christology* (Waco, TX: Baylor University Press, 2009), which pays very close attention to the narrative of Mark and the way in which it tells its story.

If you are more interested in the different ways of interpreting Mark's Gospel today, then Janice Capel Anderson and Stephen D. Moore, *Mark and Method: New Approaches in Biblical Studies*, 2nd edn (Minneapolis, MN: Augsburg Fortress, 2008), is very good.

Other resources

For the use of poetry in our Christian formation see two books by Mark Pryce, *Literary Companion to the Lectionary* (London: SPCK, 2001), and *Literary Companion for Festivals* (London: SPCK, 2003). And for an introduction to the Lectionary readings have a look at James Woodward and Leslie Houlden, *Praying the Lectionary: Prayers & Reflections for Every Week's Readings* (London: SPCK, 2007).